The (Help!) I-Don't-Have-Enough-Time Guide

to

Volunteer Management

KATHERINE NOYES CAMPBELL

AND

SUSAN J. ELLIS

With sincere thanks to Kathleen Hall and Arlene Ferris
who made time to review and strengthen our manuscript, and to all
our colleagues and friends who shared their good thinking with us.

Library of Congress Cataloging-in-Publication Data

Campbell, Katherine Noyes, 1950-
    The (Help!) I-don't-have-enough-time guide to volunteer management /
Katherine Noyes Campbell and Susan J. Ellis.
        p.   cm.
    Includes bibliographical references and index.
    ISBN 0-940576-16-3
        1. Voluntarism—United States—Management—Handbooks, manuals, etc.
2. Volunteers—Training of—United States—Handbooks, manuals, etc.
3. Work groups—United States—Management—Handbooks, manuals, etc.
I. Ellis, Susan J. II. Title.
HN90.V64C353 1995
302'.14—dc20   95-37058
                                                                CIP

Copyright © 1995 by ENERGIZE, Inc.   Second printing, 1998
                  5450 Wissahickon Avenue
                  Philadelphia, PA 19144

ISBN 0-940576-16-3

An earlier version of this book was published by ENERGIZE in 1981 under the
title, *No Excuses: The Team Approach to Volunteer Management* by Susan J. Ellis and
Katherine H. Noyes.

PRINTED IN THE UNITED STATES OF AMERICA

Contents

If you wish to make 8½"x 11" size versions of the sample forms in this book, just enlarge them using your photocopier set to the following percentages:

Preface

In 1981, when we wrote the original version of this book, *No Excuses: The Team Approach to Volunteer Management*, it was out of concern for how many volunteer managers were stretched thin—struggling to handle the demands of creating and running volunteer projects as an adjunct to other job responsibilities or on a part-time basis. Fourteen years later, the need for this book still exists, but enough has changed in the field of volunteer administration to warrant an update.

The number, quality and scope of books and other resources (including electronic forums) teaching the skills of volunteer management have increased dramatically. So it is now possible to learn from the experiences of others instead of just by trial and error. There is evidence that an expanding number of disciplines are acknowledging the contributions and potential role of volunteers, with the accompanying recognition of the need for competent leadership of volunteers. Also, people are increasingly aware that volunteer management is a career option.

It is our hope that *The (Help!) I-Don't-Have-Enough-Time Guide to Volunteer Management* will find its way into the hands of many who, although working with volunteers as part of their jobs, have not previously considered themselves to be part of the field of volunteer administration. As colleagues, we welcome you.

It is also our hope that the contents of this book will be of value to our colleagues who are unquestionably full-time in the work of directing volunteers, but who typically feel overwhelmed. Too often, the price of success in building a thriving and expanding volunteer project is limitless agency expectations without additional staff help. We understand this reality and offer the strategies in *The (Help!) Guide* to you as well.

As usual, there has been a true team approach to the writing of this book. Despite now living in different cities and having two careers going at full speed, the writing relationship we began twenty-four years ago remains unchanged. We hope it's as good for you as it is for us!

Katherine Noyes Campbell and Susan J. Ellis
Richmond and Philadelphia, 1995

i

INTRODUCTION

You've just been informed that, due to your organizational skills and warm personality, you have been given an additional responsibility: running the volunteer program. *(Aghhh!)*

The reference desk phones are ringing off the hook. There are three people standing in front of you with questions. Your monthly report on library usage is overdue. And over there, four new student volunteers are waiting to be oriented and trained. *(This is help?)*

You are running a full calendar of resident activities, dealing with individual therapy plans, organizing weekend excursions—and the holidays are fast approaching. Your message bin shows that three churches, a sorority, and the local Volunteer Center have all called in search of Christmas projects to help senior citizens. *(How will I ever find the time to manage them, too?)*

You're struggling to keep your head above water as the success of your organization's volunteer effort overwhelms you. Two hundred volunteers, working seven days a week in twenty activity areas—and administration wants the program to keep on growing. *(Wish I could clone myself—fast.)*

Can you find yourself in any of the illustrations above? Even a little bit?

The reality is that a vast number—perhaps the majority—of people responsible for leading volunteers are handling that role as one of several other professional "hats." Many people have only limited time and resources with which to do the job of volunteer administration, and therefore must find ways to handle all the job, without all the time.

This book does not necessarily promote the notion that bigger is better nor that every organization needs a full-time director of volunteers. *However,* as soon as an organization invites even one person to volunteer, it takes on the obligation to support that volunteer well. With paid workers, this is commonly understood. Hiring any staff requires basic planning and management related to work space, supervision, recordkeeping. With volunteer workers come many of the same responsibilities. In both cases, the simple fact is that adding more workers leads to expanded administrative systems. So—at some point—a small volunteer effort may evolve into a larger one, resulting in the need for more or different staffing.

In the last analysis, size is not the important issue. Of greater significance is vision. Volunteers, whether in small or large numbers, have enormous potential to further an organization's mission. If they are perceived as "add-on" helpers, you'll deal with them as add-on helpers, and they'll end up being only add-on helpers. Conversely, if you can envision the full possibilities of volunteer contributions, you'll approach the management of volunteers as resource development, and you'll end up rewarded. There is a direct correlation between the quality of attention given to volunteers and the quality of their contributions.

Before going any further, it may be helpful to clarify the term "part-timer" as used throughout this book. "Part-time" refers to the amount of time *focused on the responsibilities of running a volunteer program,* not necessarily to the number of hours you work for your organization. For the purposes of this book, it does not matter whether you are paid or you lead the volunteer effort as a volunteer yourself. Variations include:

1. You work full-time, carrying a number of job responsibilities, only one of which is management of the volunteer program/activities.

   – You carry the same type of workload as several other staff members, except for the additional responsibility of the volunteer program (i.e., you are one of many teachers or probation officers).

   – You already carry a workload unlike any other staff member, and so the additional responsibility of the volunteer program is simply one more unique role you play (i.e., you are the public relations manager or the resource development director).

   – You are the executive director/administrator and are carrying the responsibility for volunteers as an extension of your leadership of the whole organization.

2. You work on a part-time schedule, managing the volunteer program/activities as your sole responsibility during your limited hours.

3. You work full-time, managing volunteers as your sole responsibility. However:

   – Volunteers are scheduled on more than five days a week, and/or on more than eight hours a day, and/or at several locations. Therefore, by definition, you can only be there "part of the time" that the program operates.

   – The program has grown beyond your ability to manage alone.

3

– You are the director of volunteers, but have been given additional responsibilities that require you to spend "part of your time" on things other than volunteer management.

If you find yourself in variation 2 or 3, you probably self-identify with the profession of volunteer administration, whether you are a newcomer or a veteran. However, if you are among those in variation 1, for whom volunteer management is only part of what you do, you quite correctly identify with other areas of professional expertise (recreation, corrections, social work, education, health care) and view directing a volunteer program as something appended to your "regular" job.

From a practical standpoint, if you carry *any* responsibility for coordinating or supervising volunteers, *you are part of the field of volunteer administration.* You may also be a nurse, a librarian, a curator, or a probation officer, but when you are doing tasks related to volunteer leadership, you are indeed an administrator of volunteers. In short, the emphasis is on the leadership role and activities, not on how much time you devote to it. Having accepted this basic premise, the next step is to recognize—and rejoice in—how much you have in common with everyone else who directs volunteers, on a full-time or part-time, salaried or non-salaried, basis.

If this *Guide* is your first introduction to the existence of the field of volunteer management, we urge you to explore the Appendix for many helpful resources.

The (Help!) I-Don't-Have-Enough-Time Guide is based on the premise that a team approach to managing a volunteer program is a good idea, for many reasons. Put simply, the "team approach" means recruiting helpers to share the tasks of coordinating people, projects, and paper. But you delegate *authority* as well as work. This certainly is not proposed as a quick fix for the problem of too many responsibilities and not enough time. In fact, it will take time to plan for and build the best team structure for you. Once in place, however, a management team will indeed allow you to share the work, be in more than one place at once, and feel some relief from the burden of carrying the whole weight of the volunteer program alone.

There are many ideas presented in this book and the cumulative effect may be formidable at first. But many of the suggestions can be implemented singly and still make a big difference in your day-to-day operations. Please feel free to pick and choose what speaks to your needs and seems the most do-able.

While the focus of this book is on part-timers, the strategy of team management is valid for any volunteer program. The team approach fosters shared ownership of volunteer involvement by including many people, both paid and volunteer, in the work it takes to make it happen. As volunteer activities expand, the demands of leadership expand as well. No matter what the size of a volunteer effort, there comes a point at which the workload as well as expectations exceed the present level of staff support. The techniques in *The (Help!) Guide* apply at all stages of growth.

1

RECOGNIZING YOUR ROLE

This *Guide* is designed to help you step back and examine the responsibility you have been given to lead volunteers. This process begins with understanding the basic elements of effective volunteer management. In these pages you will not find information on how to do recruitment, screening, training or recordkeeping; rather, you will explore a practical strategy for adapting your role so that all these tasks can get done within the constraints of your available time. If you do need to build your basic skills in volunteer program development, the Appendix will direct you to helpful resources—both books and organizations.

The basic task elements of effective volunteer administration remain constant and must all be accomplished, regardless of the time available to do them. Unfortunately, too many people are given (and accept) the responsibility for directing volunteers without a full understanding of what the job entails. Even with a written job description, major functions are all too often reduced to single words such as "recruit," "interview," "train," "recognize." This is based on two assumptions: 1) each function is relatively simple, and 2) everyone knows the work that each implies. Both assumptions are false.

The revelation that the assignment has been grossly under-estimated may hit home only after you have accepted the role. Then you find yourself looking for shortcuts, especially if you are directing volunteers only on a part-time basis. For example, if you are assigned to manage the program during 20 hours a week ("half-time"), you will soon discover that you cannot do only "half" the tasks of recruitment or "half" the tasks of supervision! If you try to ignore certain aspects of the job, the consequences will haunt you. Quite a dilemma.

Perhaps the most effective way to reconcile the demands of the job with the time available in which to do them is to *share the tasks with others*. This "team approach" may seem simple and obvious as you read about it, and yet can be quite challenging to actually do. On the following pages you will find concrete suggestions and strategies for ensuring that you do not have to do your job alone. And, yes, the team approach also works if you are a full-time Director of Volunteer Services trying to handle the demands and expectations of an expanding program.

Regardless of your situation or the strategies you ultimately adopt, your success will be predicated on three important points:

1. You understand the scope of the job.

Chapter 3 provides a detailed list of volunteer management tasks. As you read it, edit it by adding or deleting items to make it relevant to your own situation and the unique aspects of your setting. The goal is to develop a comprehensive definition of what needs to happen in order to effectively mobilize and direct volunteer resources within your organization. Though the length of this list may seem overwhelming at first, facing it as a "known quantity" is immeasurably better than continually being surprised by the number of tasks concealed behind general phrases like "recruit new volunteers."

2. You believe in the value of volunteer involvement.

In addition to specific tasks, there is another major factor in assuring successful volunteer management: attitude. This is a person-to-person job directly influenced by the amount of honest commitment you feel to volunteerism. Such commitment, in turn, may be influenced by how you came to hold the position. Did you actively seek the role? Did you "fall into it" by accident? Were you assigned to it ("anointed")? Those who enter the field of volunteer administration by accident often accept leadership of a volunteer program as a temporary stepping stone to something else, such as a promotion, direct client supervision, etc. The "anointed" often recognize that they may have been designated rather arbitrarily, and see the assignment as auxiliary to (and of lower priority than) their "real" jobs.

Regardless of how you came to be in charge of volunteers, the challenge is to cultivate the attitudes necessary for success:

- Belief in the value and power of volunteerism.

- Recognition of people's potential capabilities, rather than their formal credentials.

- Desire to make the program work to its fullest potential.

- Openness to tapping a variety of volunteers (different ages, backgrounds, ideas, etc.).

- Willingness to stand up for the rights of volunteers.

- Enjoyment of working with volunteers.

3. You are committed to the team approach because it benefits *the organization* as much as it benefits you.

On the following pages the phrase "management team" will be used repeatedly to refer to the cooperative approach to leading volunteers. You will still be in charge, but with the benefit of shared responsibility as specific tasks are delegated to others. The program will be stronger because it will have gained the input of ideas and perspectives in addition to your own. You and your co-workers will share both problems and successes, resulting in real joint ownership of the results. You will avoid the trap of isolation which often comes when you are the only one who understands the job. And neither you nor the organization will fall prey to the "solo syndrome"—the perception that the success or failure of volunteer involvement rests on only one person's shoulders. Thus, from the double perspective of both time management and program development, recruiting a team to share your leadership role makes a lot of sense.

2

MAPPING THE BOUNDARIES

Although you may have grasped the magnitude of the job of directing volunteers, it is quite likely that no one else in your organization has! Do not be surprised at the recurring question: "What exactly do you do in that job?" It is up to you to guide your organization towards a realistic assessment of how you and volunteers fit into the overall picture. You should feel comfortable in your role as *resident expert in volunteerism* and in recommending the type of structure and support necessary for a successful program.

Whether you are just starting out or have been in the job for years, you need to ask for planning time with your organization's executive staff and/or board—those who can make policy decisions and enforce them. Often, volunteers have been incorporated into the organization in a rather random and haphazard way, without much deliberate planning. Your leadership position may have evolved in the same way. So it is never too early nor too late to develop ground rules acceptable to everyone. Furthermore, taking this proactive step will help you avoid feeling "victimized" by the situation, and will demonstrate your desire to manage volunteer resources in a way that benefits the entire organization.

When you plan your meeting with the people at the top, the agenda should include questions such as the following:

Why do we want volunteers?

This is not a frivolous—nor easily answered—question. It is the cornerstone of developing a working philosophy about volunteers to translate into a meaningful program. Just as a mission statement articulates why an organization exists, so too must you be able to express, in concrete terms, why volunteers are a desirable part of your operation. Tradition or lack of funds are not, in and of themselves, good enough reasons, for these severely limit the ways in which we view potential roles for volunteers.

One useful way to approach this issue is to pose the question: If we had all the money in the world to do the work of our organization, would we still want volunteers involved? This usually invites some discussion uncovering many of the unique characteristics of volunteers with direct bearing on the organization's mission. Even if volunteers have been involved for a long time, the answers to this question can be surprising and worth discovering or reaffirming. (For an in-depth discussion of this issue, see *From the Top Down: The Executive Role in Volunteer Program Success* by Susan J. Ellis, Energize, 1996.)

What is our vision for the volunteer program?

What will be the size and scope of volunteer involvement a year or two from now? In ten years? It is important to clarify such expectations because they are directly related to the amount of time allotted to direct volunteers. If you can only devote a few hours to volunteers, program growth will be limited. Conversely, if a larger or more complex program is desired, consideration may have to be given to expanding your available time. Or, is the agency willing to cap growth if your time must remain limited? Discuss the adaptation that might be necessary as the ratio of volunteers to salaried staff changes (up or down). It may also be helpful to mention that growth in the number of volunteers requires an increased investment by the organization, not only in terms of your time but also in terms of space, supplies, shared power, etc.

What are our expectations of volunteers?

What are the goals and objectives for involving volunteers? What exactly do we want them to accomplish? How many volunteers are anticipated at any given time? Bringing what skills? The answers to these questions will, of course, be determined in large part by the results of needs assessments and the development of volunteer job descriptions.

What does "part-time" mean?

If you are assigned to lead volunteers on a part-time basis, it is crucial to define time expectations as well. Exactly how much time is "part-time"? Can you block out specific times of the week to be designated for the volunteer program? If applicable, will your other responsibilities be reduced to allow for this? (Something has to go.) Will you have a flexible schedule for evening and weekend meetings, external speaking engagements and training sessions? Try to give specific examples of how you see the demands on your time, rather than assuming that top administrators understand why scheduling can be so important and complex. Remember, also, that you are building the case for a team approach to the job; thus it may be appropriate to mention that constraints on your time have implications for how other members of the organization can assist and participate in program management tasks.

What is my title?

No matter which leadership scenario applies to you, you must have a title that appropriately represents your role with the volunteer program. It is worth giving some thought to which words will be most effective in terms of your setting, as there are many variations and options being used today: Coordinator of Volunteers, Director of Volunteer Resources/Services, Community Resources Director, Volunteer Program Manager, Outreach Coordinator, Member Resources Chair. Whatever your choice, it is critical that your title refer to your volunteer-related function in some way. Without a title that specifically designates you as the person responsible for volunteers, you may find your various roles blurring together in everyone's mind.

If you are salaried, clarify that you are asking for an operational (working) title. Your on-the-books payroll title does not matter as long as you can present yourself to the public, sign letters, etc., with a title that indicates leadership of volunteers. One approach is to add to your current title, as in "Director of Activities and Volunteers" or "Coordinator of Volunteers and In-Home Services." Another option is to simply adopt two titles, using each when appropriate.

If you yourself are a volunteer, it is even more vital to have your title agreed upon by the organization. You deserve the respect and clout that come with being identified as "Director of Volunteers" (or any variation thereof). Your leadership role is verified by your title, allowing you to represent the organization officially in matters related to volunteers.

In either case, your title is one of the important boundary lines to be clearly drawn to avoid confusion of roles, especially when dealing with the public.

What is the chain of command?

For your own sake and the sake of volunteers, it is important to establish a chain of command that is workable and understood by all. You must have access to the decision-makers in your organization since there will always be policy questions to be answered. (If you are already the executive director or the top person in charge, this will be easy!) The "higher up" your supervisor, the better. Volunteers need to feel that you are directly tied in to the organization's administration or else they will suspect (correctly!) they have no effective voice. Similarly, employees also need to know that you, and therefore volunteers, have access to top administration.

The issue of your position in the organization hierarchy can be further complicated if you have other responsibilities in addition to volunteer management. Consider the possibility that your volunteer management role may require a different chain of command than the one which governs your other functions. Your work in In-Home Services may be monitored by the Social Work Supervisor but, for your work in coordinating volunteers, you may need to report to the Executive Director. It is better to explore this issue and reach agreement now, rather than wait until a crisis is at hand. Be aware, too, that this has implications for your relationship with your current direct supervisor. What criteria will be used to evaluate your job performance in both arenas, who will assess each piece, and who will assess your ability to do two jobs at once?!

If many volunteers will be supervised on a daily basis by persons other than you, you also need to define your role as liaison. When should someone come to you instead of his or her supervisor? When should a supervisor seek your help with a volunteer? If a volunteer feels s/he has been treated unfairly, what process do you want followed? If someone disagrees with you, who is next in line to handle the concern?

Another variation that may affect you is the existence of an independent, self-led volunteer group such as an auxiliary or "friends" group. What is your role as liaison to this group? Who has final authority? Do these volunteers have direct access to top administration or does communication go through you? Who will be held accountable for this group's activities?

What are my priorities and do you understand my limits?

Commitment to having effective volunteer involvement is demonstrated by an organizational decision to allow you to give the volunteer program priority at certain times each day and week. The attitude cannot be "fit this in when you find the time." You must deliberately make time. There will inevitably be demands pulling you into other work, but volunteers must be seen as equally important as everything else, not as the function that can always be postponed.

It is important that everyone in the organization recognize that, when you are wearing your volunteer coordinator hat, your priority at that moment must be volunteers. Therefore, you cannot drop everything because something arises related to your other job responsibilities. For example, when you are in the middle of an interview with a prospective volunteer, you cannot take calls from clients or board members.

In addition, it is very healthy to reach an understanding with everyone about your need to prioritize requests for assistance and periodically say "no." With limited time available you cannot simultaneously develop six different recruitment plans for six new volunteer assignments, or conduct a volunteer recognition event in the same week as the state auditors are due.

In order to protect yourself, there needs to be agreement from the top as to how to set priorities at any given time. This will give you the justification for selecting one type of action over another. Second, this once again provides an opportunity to discuss how certain requests can be delegated to another member of your management team; you can make the connection between shared ownership and increased results.

It is a lot easier to set limits early than it is to stem the tide of unrealistic requests later on. But if you are trying to re-train colleagues who are overly demanding, put your concerns on the table and then be firmly consistent in refusing to be overwhelmed. It may also help to explain exactly what is involved in meeting certain time-consuming requests, responding again to the fact that your colleagues may think the task is simpler than it is. For example, if co-workers come to understand the multi-step process in recruiting volunteers, they'll be less likely to expect results overnight.

What are the volunteer program's budget and resources?

Trite but true: volunteers are not free help. You need to develop an appropriate budget for necessary expenses, ranging from printing and postage to transportation reimbursement and insurance. Though it may take some time to arrange for sufficient funds to cover such things, one way an organization demonstrates its commitment to volunteers is to acknowledge that these expenses are real and plan for them in the overall organizational budget.

Do not underestimate your need for other basic support resources such as: work space for volunteers, including places in which to store work in progress; sufficient telephones and/or computers; adequate office supplies; coat racks; access to rest rooms; etc. Individually these items may seem minor, but they contribute substantially to effective volunteer involvement. They also represent hidden costs (along with the cost of staff time in supervising volunteers), which should be made visible.

If the notion of an itemized budget for the volunteer program is new, you may have to advocate for this over a period of time. Gather evidence as to what costs have been incurred in the past, and then add in other items which are basic to the operation of the program. Some volunteer administrators have found it helpful to go ahead and prepare a program budget even if they have not been asked to do so. They then present it to their top administration at the time when the agency budget is being developed, offering it as a tool to help their bosses be prepared for the year ahead, rather than be faced with unexpected expenses. The simple act of itemizing specific support costs for volunteer involvement can be enlightening for everyone—especially if it is done in a way that demonstrates cost effectiveness and return on investment.

How often will we schedule status reviews?

It is useful to build in periodic re-examination sessions with your administrators to assess whether and how the volunteer program is changing over time. Is it necessary to adjust your job description to allow you more time with the volunteer program? How is your management team doing? Do you need additional paid assistance? Are the original goals and objectives for the volunteer program still relevant? Have volunteers been planned into new projects? Such a status review is consistent with recommended periodic program evaluations.

Furthermore, it is important to pose these questions consciously to avoid the snowball effect of allowing volunteers to increase in number and degree of involvement without adapting the leadership structure accordingly. Whether part-time or full-time, you may be taken for granted as the program grows, based on the assumption that you're doing fine and nothing needs to be adjusted. The price of success will be burnout and an overwhelming workload unless you keep presenting your changing needs and situation.

Another reason for regular review is to keep your role visible and understood by those in charge. Volunteer managers who do not initiate discussion of the progress and needs of the volunteer program are the most susceptible to being underfunded—or even cut—when a budget crunch occurs. Once again, being proactive will yield real benefits in the long run.

A word of caution: the question of appropriate staffing for the growth of volunteer involvement is separate from your personal career goals. It is possible that you do not want to pursue full-time volunteer management as your job and prefer to focus on your chosen profession of social work, teaching, occupational therapy, information science, or whatever. In this case, your responsibility is to help your organization recognize when the volunteer program deserves full-time staff attention and to encourage the hiring of a trained volunteer manager so that you can return to your own career path.

How will we assure organization-wide involvement?

As already mentioned, the designation of one individual (you) to lead your organization's volunteer effort does not relieve everyone else of responsibility for supporting and actively assisting the program. *Everyone*—from administration to maintenance, salaried or not—must demonstrate respect for, faith in, and enthusiasm about volunteers. You cannot maintain an upbeat atmosphere and motivation all by yourself, especially if you are a part-time director of volunteers. Your organization's commitment to welcoming community involvement must be evident at all times. However, such support does not happen overnight, and you may encounter resistance to volunteers from some staff. Furthermore, your co-workers need continual opportunities to provide input, hear about program progress, and learn about your job. You can work to develop positive attitudes and meet these needs by requesting the following from your executive:

- regular reporting time at staff meetings;

- opportunities to train paid and key volunteer staff in techniques of volunteer supervision;

- that supervision of volunteers be made part of staff job descriptions and evaluation criteria;

- permission to involve staff in recruitment, training, recognition activities, etc.;

- open discussion of ideas and suggestions for the volunteer program.

All of these activities will demonstrate the philosophy that volunteers are not "yours," but are an integral part of the entire organization, affecting everyone. Chapter 4 will discuss specific ways various employees can work with you to use their special skills on behalf of volunteer program success. However, you should not be put in the position of asking for help from colleagues as "a favor" to you. It is up to your administrators to establish and reinforce that such cooperation is necessary.

Mapping the boundaries is an important responsibility— it comes with the territory of leading volunteers. Do not expect or wait for your higher-ups to define things for you. On their own, they may not. They may assume that everything is fine because you have not told them otherwise. As hard as it may be for you to initiate discussion about the sticky issues presented in this chapter, it is to your advantage to do so in the long run. If you avoid these issues, you are reinforcing the notion that volunteer management is quick and easy.

Being willing to raise these questions demonstrates your professionalism and desire to be a competent leader of volunteers. Remember, too, that the answers are critical in supporting all the volunteers and affect the rest of the organization, as well as yourself. Take the lead.

3

TASK ANALYSIS AND
DELEGATION

When you are asked to lead a volunteer program, you are given a mandate to utilize people creatively—whether they come from the community at large or from within the organization itself. You need to cultivate the ability to recognize the full range of possible ways people can become involved in all aspects of your organization. The same imagination you show in developing direct-service volunteer assignments should extend to developing new ways for people to participate on your management team. Since you do not have the time to do everything yourself, you must delegate specific parts of your job to others.

As stated in Chapter 1, it is critical that you fully understand the various elements of volunteer program management before asking others to help with specific pieces of the job. It is therefore helpful to consider all the possible activities that contribute to the effective utilization of volunteer resources, and analyze how they relate to your particular situation.

The following Task Analysis is designed to help you with this process. The *functions*, designated by Roman numerals, are major cluster areas of the job of running a volunteer program. The *responsibilities* outlined A, B, C, etc. are the key activities in each function (and are what would usually appear in a regular job

21

description). The *tasks* listed under each responsibility as 1, 2, 3, etc. are just *some* of the basic steps necessary to accomplish each responsibility. It is precisely these tasks which need to be identified both to understand your job and to select assignments to delegate to team members. Despite its length, this is a generalized Task Analysis, and details will vary depending on your organization and setting.

The Task Analysis can also be used to educate others in your organization if you feel they do not fully understand what needs to happen in order to mobilize and utilize volunteer resources effectively. Consider sharing the Analysis with your boss, board members, fellow staff, and key volunteer leaders. It can also be a valuable tool for developing or refining your own job description.[1]

Take time to review the Analysis more than once. The first time, make sure you consider if all of your work is included. Are there other tasks which need to be added? Delete the tasks for which you are not responsible. Jot notes in the margin.

VOLUNTEER MANAGEMENT TASK ANALYSIS

I. PROGRAM PLANNING AND ADMINISTRATION

A. Assess/analyze agency and client needs for assistance.
1. Design questionnaires, survey forms, etc. to determine areas where assistance is needed.
2. Interview (or otherwise contact) employees, administration, volunteers, clients/consumers, etc.
3. Tabulate results of interviews/surveys; summarize findings.
4. Research models of other volunteer programs in similar settings.

B. Articulate a vision for volunteer involvement in the organization.
1. Develop a written statement presenting the organization's philosophy about volunteer involvement.
2. Identify the key values guiding the volunteer program: diversity; mutual respect; confidentiality; etc.
3. Determine the organizational definition of "volunteer" in terms of the scope of community resources available, such as: student service-learning programs; alternative sentencing programs; corporate employee programs; etc.
4. Consider the range of ways volunteers can be asked to participate, including: assisting paid staff; working independently; as technical advisors, etc.

C. Develop program goals and objectives.
1. Determine possible long-range and short-range program goals, using data from the needs assessment.
2. Develop measurable goals for what volunteers will accomplish and criteria for evaluating effectiveness.
3. Review these with administration and integrate into overall agency planning.

D. Design volunteer assignments.
1. Determine volunteer job categories based on needs assessment and program goals.

23

2. Work with paid staff to develop volunteer job descriptions.
3. Write job descriptions for volunteers who will be helping to manage the volunteer program.
4. Review set of job descriptions periodically with supervisors and volunteers carrying those responsibilities, and revise as necessary.
5. Write function descriptions for committees and organized groups.
6. Define the role of program advisors.

E. Develop risk management procedures and strategies.
1. Understand legal and insurance issues as they relate to volunteers.
2. Obtain adequate insurance coverage for volunteers.
3. Identify specific areas of potential risks and develop policies, training, and other strategies to limit such risks.

F. Coordinate schedules.
1. Plan overall work schedule for volunteer assignments.
2. Coordinate with salaried staff as needed.
3. Track attendance patterns with sign-in sheets and other systems of monitoring volunteer services. (See Function VIII: Recordkeeping.)

G. Set policies and procedures.
1. Review agency policies and procedures; consult with administration and supervisory staff about any requirements and rules affecting volunteers.
2. Draft overall volunteer program policies and procedures; obtain approval.
3. Determine policies and procedures for specific volunteer assignments.
4. Develop and maintain a volunteer program procedures manual.

H. Manage budget.
1. Determine annual budget needs and convey them to administration.
2. Authorize budget expenditures.

3. Develop a petty cash system, a system for reimbursing volunteers, and any other necessary fiscal procedures.
4. Solicit in-kind donations for the volunteer program.
5. Plan and implement fundraising events for the volunteer program.

I. Meet support needs.
1. Arrange for adequate space, furniture, equipment and supplies to support volunteers.
2. Meet with supervisory staff to determine where (space) volunteers will work.
3. Order uniforms, nametags, etc., as appropriate; develop distribution system.
4. Develop support services for volunteers as necessary, such as car pools, child care, etc.

J. Advocate for volunteers.
1 Represent the volunteers' point of view to the organization.
2. Inform agency staff about issues related to volunteers, such as insurance coverage, tax deductions, enabling funds.
3. Initiate action on such issues, both within the organization and in support of community efforts or legislation.

K. Develop new projects.
1. Participate in agency-wide program planning to assure proper involvement of volunteers.
2. Gather ideas for new volunteer projects and program expansion.
3. Propose and justify such ideas.
4. Initiate pilot projects to test ideas.
5. Participate in related resource finding and funding activities.

L. Develop professional skills.
1. Read professional volunteerism books and periodicals.
2. Attend volunteer management workshops and conferences.
3. Network with other directors of volunteers through professional associations.

M. Other:

II. RECRUITMENT AND PUBLIC RELATIONS

A. Plan recruitment strategies.
1. Identify the types of volunteers and/or skills needed for each volunteer job.
2. Brainstorm (and then prioritize) available sources of potential volunteers suited to each job description.
3. Solicit suggestions and contacts from employees, present and past volunteers, family and friends, consumers, etc.

B. Develop recruitment and media relations materials.
1. Write wording for a range of general and targeted flyers, posters, brochures, etc.
2. Work with a graphic artist to design recruitment materials; coordinate printing.
3. Write and schedule (request) public service announcements on radio and television.
4. Write and send press releases.
5. Distribute/post materials at appropriate public sites, including electronic networks/bulletin boards.
6. Develop slide shows and other audio-visual materials to support oral presentations.
7. Create an exhibit/display for multiple uses.

C. Handle public speaking and personal contacts.
1. Contact leaders of groups of potential volunteers and arrange to speak to members.
2. Accept speaking engagements requested by community groups.
3. Seek out and do local radio, television and newspaper interviews and talk shows.
4. Explain program needs in one-to-one meetings with key resource people.
5. Develop corps of "program representatives" trained to speak on behalf of the program.

D. Manage ongoing recruitment efforts.
1. Maintain regular contact with frequent sources of volun-

teers (e.g., schools, churches, civic groups).
2. Register volunteer opportunities with all referral sources such as Volunteer Centers.
3. Work with staff to insure that all agency public relations materials include mention of volunteer opportunities.
4. Enlist the help of salaried staff and current volunteers in locating new volunteers.

E. Other:

III. INTERVIEWING AND SCREENING

A. Prepare for applicants.
1. Design application form to be used by all prospective volunteers.
2. Develop interview format appropriate to staff schedules, program setting and agency needs.
3. Brief switchboard, receptionists, and secretaries that members of the public will be calling and coming in for appointments.

B. Conduct interviews.
1. Schedule interviews with all prospective volunteers.
2. Obtain and review completed application forms.
3. Describe various volunteer opportunities, using job descriptions, and discuss performance expectations.

C. Screen.
1. Screen out candidates inappropriate for the organization or having skills that could be better used in another setting by referring them to other community volunteer programs.
2. Adapt job descriptions to unique skills of prospective volunteers.
3. Create special assignments when feasible.
4. Develop procedure for accepting an applicant conditionally (such as probationary period), if not certain as to her/his appropriateness.

5. Conduct background checks as required or desired.

D. Assign volunteers.

1. Tentatively match appropriate applicants to currently-available assignments and time slots.
2. Arrange for further screening, if necessary, by immediate supervisors of the assignment being considered.
3. Make final decision to accept and schedule starting date.

E. Facilitate group volunteer involvement.

1. Identify potential projects/assignments for organized groups of volunteers to handle independently.
2. Meet with leaders of prospective groups of volunteers and speak with members.
3. Establish written guidelines for supervising work and communications.

F. Other:

IV. ORIENTATION AND TRAINING

A. Develop an orientation program for all volunteers, regardless of assignment.

1. Plan agenda.
2. Arrange for tour of facility.
3. Invite or videotape speakers (including key salaried staff, administration, board).
4. Prepare informational materials to distribute to new volunteers.
5. Schedule and conduct sessions as needed.
6. Design individually-tailored orientation for specialized (one-shot or short-term) events or group projects.

B. Offer staff development.

1. Identify level of expertise among salaried staff in working with volunteers; identify positive and negative attitudes.
2. Meet individually with any staff resistant to volunteers, in an attempt to discuss the situation and resolve it.

3. Offer periodic staff seminars on volunteer management.
4. In staff meetings, report on volunteer program progress and concerns.
5. Participate in the orientation of new employees so that they learn about the organization's volunteers.

C. Design initial training plan.
1. Work with supervisors to design specific training for each volunteer assignment.
2. Assist with the scheduling of training.
3. Monitor that each volunteer receives training.
4. Develop and conduct initial training for volunteers directly working under volunteer office supervision.
5. Involve experienced volunteers in assisting newcomers.

D. Develop in-service training options.
1. Solicit interest in and needs for in-service training from volunteers and salaried staff.
2. Plan annual training schedule.
3. Prepare for sessions; invite speakers and resource people.
4. Conduct or moderate sessions.
5. Evaluate training plan and results.
6. Arrange for volunteers to attend special events, workshops, tours, etc.

E. Prepare manuals and handbooks.
1. Gather information for inclusion in manual.
2. Review sample manuals from other programs.
3. Discuss possible contents with volunteers and agency staff.
4. Write manual.
5. Design appearance and arrange for printing.

F. Other:

V. SUPERVISION

A. Handle direct supervision.
1. Meet regularly with members of volunteer management team.
2. Establish supervision plan for volunteers assigned

directly to the volunteer office.
3. Maintain regular contact with off-site or off-hour (evening, weekend) volunteers.
4. Supervise any paid staff directly assigned to the volunteer program.

B. Handle indirect supervision.
1. Communicate regularly with those staff who directly supervise volunteers.
2. Monitor that volunteers are utilized appropriately, with tasks suited to abilities.
3. Assure that supervisors are accessible to volunteers and are maintaining a regular schedule of supervisory contact.

C. Be a liaison.
1. Serve as "third party" moderator to resolve any problems arising between volunteers and salaried staff members, or among volunteers themselves.
2. Be available to all volunteers and salaried staff as next step in the "chain of command."

D. Manage individual volunteer performance assessment.
1. Develop a plan for periodic assessment of volunteers' progress, achievements, areas requiring further training, etc.
2. Train supervisors to conduct periodic, mutual evaluations in a constructive way with all volunteers assigned to them.
3. Review all such evaluative reports.
4. Evaluate performance of volunteers assigned directly to the volunteer office.
5. Insure that volunteers do self-evaluation and have opportunity to evaluate their training and supervision.

E. Other:

VI. MOTIVATION AND RECOGNITION

A. Assure ongoing volunteer motivation and appreciation.

1. Promote agency-wide atmosphere of welcome, courtesy, motivation and productivity.
2. Suggest ways for salaried staff to demonstrate appreciation of volunteers on a day-to-day basis.
3. Establish methods for volunteers to express concerns and offer suggestions.
4. Promote communication among program participants through such devices as a program newsletter, bulletin boards, and staff meetings.

B. Conduct recognition activities.

1. Plan formal recognition of all volunteer services, such as annual events or awards.
2. Identify those volunteers eligible for special recognition.
3. Thank those employees who contribute to the volunteer program.
4. Write letters of reference for volunteers when requested.
5. Involve top agency personnel in recognizing volunteer contributions.
6. Assure ongoing, informal expressions of appreciation to volunteers.

C. Develop "career ladders" for volunteers.

1. Review all assignments regularly to see that volunteers continue to be challenged and enjoy their activities.
2. Design advanced-level tasks for those volunteers earning and desiring more difficult (responsible, sophisticated) work.
3. Utilize experienced volunteers in special projects, in program evaluation and planning, and as recruiters and trainers of new volunteers.

D. Other:

31

VII. PROGRAM EVALUATION

A. Conduct regular program evaluation.
1. Develop a plan for program evaluation; form an evaluation team.
2. Design questionnaires, surveys, etc.; recruit and train interviewers.
3. Solicit input from all program constituents.
4. Analyze data and develop concrete plan of action based on evaluation results.
5. Report evaluation results to all program constituents and integrate into agency planning.

B. Assess ongoing progress in all program components.
1. Keep informed about progress in all areas.
2. Track pilot projects carefully; review at scheduled intervals.
3. Conduct "exit interviews" with volunteers leaving the organization to gain insights into areas for improvement in assignments and management.

C. Other:

VIII. RECORDKEEPING AND REPORTING

A. Develop a comprehensive volunteer recordkeeping system.
1. Determine data needs for program management, risk management, and to document the accomplishments of volunteers.
2. Review agency records and reporting systems, to see where volunteer data could be integrated.
3. Design forms and develop procedures to gather data, including computerization as feasible.
4. Train volunteers and salaried staff to provide data accurately and on time.

B. Maintain system.
1. Record data in an accurate, up-to-date and accessible manner.

    2. Follow up forms or reports not turned in.

    3. Keep records on own activities as Director of Volunteers.

C. Develop reports.
    1. Write monthly and annual reports, giving both statistics and descriptive narratives.
    2. Distribute reports to all program constituents, as well as to administration.
    3. Prepare special reports upon request.

D. Other:

IX. OTHER RESPONSIBILITIES

A. Participate in agency fundraising events, coordinating volunteer assistance.

B. Solicit in-kind donations to assist agency services.

C. Represent the organization at community functions; represent the organization to visiting community members.

D. Provide technical assistance to other agency volunteer efforts, such as board development, working with auxiliaries, etc.

E. Promote volunteerism as an avenue for personal and professional growth, and as a resource for addressing community problems.

F. Other:

Now that you have a better understanding of what your job entails, you are ready to consider who could assist in getting the work done. Review the Analysis again, this time considering the following questions for each function and task:

- Is this *currently being done* by someone else in the organization? Is this working well, or are there problems?

- Is this something I *like* to do? Would it be hard for me to turn this over to someone else, or would I just as soon have someone else do it?

- Can I do it well? Do I have the *necessary skills*, or would it be done better (or faster) by someone with greater expertise than I?

- How does this task fit with my *current work schedule?* Does it have to be done at a specific time of day? How does this fit with the requirements of my other job responsibilities?

- How *frequently* does this have to be done? Continuously? Weekly? Monthly? Annually?

- Is this task something I am *required* to do, given agency policies, regulations, or law?

- Should this task be done by one *individual,* or could it be done by *several people,* or a *group?*

The answers to these questions will let you begin to identify which tasks are the easiest and most logical to delegate to someone else—the members of your management team. A tool to help with this process is the "Delegation Potential Sheet" on the next page. Make a Sheet for each function or task with which you feel you need help, breaking it down further into a sequence of specific activities. For each activity, consider the implications of timing, authority, and necessary skills, so that you can decide if that activity can be delegated. Then identify possible helpers. Be careful of your assumptions about what you can and cannot delegate, and remember it is possible to exercise quality control even if others are

Delegation Potential Sheet

Job Function/Task: _____

Activity Analysis (the steps of the work, in sequence)	Amount of time needed; deadline	Do I have to be involved personally? Why?	Can it be delegated? fully / in part	Skills Needed	Potential Helpers

doing some of the work (more on this later).

There are two more ways to approach job design for your management team, using the Volunteer Management Task Analysis. You can seek people to handle a complete cluster of tasks within a particular function, such as taking charge of in-service training or coordinating student intern placements. Or, you can recruit people because they have skills applicable to several functions. For example, a writer can help you develop recruitment materials, a volunteer handbook, a newsletter and press releases. Here is a list of necessary skills or expertise implied by the Task Analysis. Note how the same skill can be applied to several different functions or tasks.

Writing
Forms Development
Group Dynamics
Interviewing/Research
Survey Design
Statistics
Long-Range Planning
Fiscal Management
Knowledge of Community
Art Work/Graphics
Printing
Advertising/Marketing
Photography
Public Speaking
Computer Technology
Training Design
Adult Education
Event Planning
Catering
Career Guidance
Editing
Bookkeeping/Accounting
Fundraising/Resource Development
Public Relations

Counseling
Organizing/Scheduling/Coordinating
Media Relations

As this chapter demonstrates, the responsibility of managing a volunteer program is inherently complex, demanding a range of "left brain" and "right brain" talents. Success in the role comes from combining great human relations skills with strong administrative and technical abilities. Very few people possess all these attributes. So even if you have sufficient time to do the work, there are still good reasons to reach out to other talented people. Here is one more way that a team effort benefits you, volunteers, and the whole organization.

---

[1] The Association for Volunteer Administration has developed a professional certification program for managers of volunteers. It is based on a comprehensive list of "competencies" considered the core components of effective volunteer program leadership. This is another way of looking at your role, complementing the Volunteer Management Task Analysis presented here.

4

FINDING YOUR MANAGEMENT TEAM: INSIDE

Now that you have a clear sense of what needs to be done and which tasks are best suited for delegation to others, you are ready to begin recruiting your management team members. This chapter presents ideas on potential resources within your organization, and how they can be used to help you handle various activities. The next chapter explores external community resources. The size and structure of your organization will, of course, determine which of the workers discussed here are available to you. Even with a small staff, these suggestions should stimulate your creativity as you explore ways to involve colleagues working on site with you.

Experienced Volunteers

Experienced volunteers who have been with your organization for at least a few months bring firsthand knowledge of what it is like to be a volunteer in your setting—something no one else can provide. While it is a fallacy to assume that all volunteers want to be "promoted" out of whatever assignment they presently enjoy doing, most people are willing to assist in extra ways occasionally. It is flattering to be asked to do a special job in recognition of demonstrated skills and long volunteer service. It can be particularly productive to form a task force of two to five volunteers and ask them to make recommendations on a specific aspect of the program. Experienced volunteers can also help by:

- Orienting new volunteers and selecting in-service training topics and speakers.

- Buddying up with new volunteers, both initially as a training experience and then as on-going support.

- Planning and conducting a special event.

- Sharing an otherwise untapped skill, such as taking photographs or writing a newsletter article.

- Serving as a "consultant" for volunteer program decisions such as forms design, evaluation studies, recognition planning, and policy development.

- Assisting in recruitment, especially in relation to other organizations to which they, family members or friends belong; doing public speaking on behalf of the volunteer program.

- Assisting in the recognition of supportive salaried staff.

- Helping to find funds for the volunteer program (both in terms of grants and money-raising events), especially for reimbursing volunteers' out-of-pocket costs.

Volunteers should be given the choice of taking a "leave of absence" from their regular assignment to do the special task, or of giving additional time until the special task is completed.

Secretaries

It is quite possible that you do not have a full-time secretary assigned to you. You may be working with a clerical pool whose time is divided among many staff members, or with one overworked secretary whom you share with one or more other staff. Even if you are fortunate enough to have a clerical support person all your own, by definition that person, too, may have to divide her/his time between the work generated by the volunteer program and that of your "other" job functions. No one is sitting around waiting for your volunteer-related typing, forms, and phone calls!

Nevertheless, secretaries are an invaluable part of the volunteer management team, provided their role is clearly and mutually defined. For many clerical workers, the opportunity to participate in administering a volunteer project is a welcome change from daily routine and can even be a way to demonstrate talents previously untapped by the agency. The trick is to find the right person who sincerely wants such involvement, rather than one who will feel put upon by these new demands. The reluctant helper will only transfer her/his resentment or indifference to the volunteers—which is worse than no help at all. (Is it feasible to "put out a call" throughout the organization, asking who is interested in this challenging opportunity?)

Once you have found the right secretary, it is important to outline together exactly what tasks related to volunteers will be handled by this member of your team. Some good possibilities are:

- Typing correspondence, forms, memos, and anything else related to volunteer recruitment, recognition, and management. Keep in mind that an involved secretary can be your team expert in designing appropriate formats for program materials since s/he understands the possibilities and limitations of available computer software, copying machines, and other equipment.

- Sending out form letters and brochures in response to inquiries about the volunteer program, and keeping track of them.

- Making appointments for you to meet with potential volunteers.

- Greeting prospective volunteers prior to your interview

with them and giving them the application form to complete.

- Setting up folders, index cards, and other records for each new volunteer (either manually or by computer). Once you have designed your basic recordkeeping system (with input from your secretary) you can determine which pieces of it s/he will be responsible for maintaining. (For more information on this subject, see *Proof Positive: Developing Significant Volunteer Recordkeeping Systems* by Susan J. Ellis and Katherine H. Noyes, Energize, 1990.)

- Collecting and re-stocking timesheets, volunteer sign-in logs, etc.

- Following up on volunteers who have been absent or who have not been submitting requested reports.

Depending on the capabilities of your secretary, the size of the volunteer program, and the available work space, you might want to recruit volunteer clerical assistants. Ideally, these volunteers should be directly supervised by your secretary. Good reasons for this arrangement are:

- You do not have to be in the office whenever the volunteer clerical assistants are. The secretary, who rarely has appointments out of the office, will provide consistent work assignments and supervision.

- All clerical work can be coordinated by the same person, avoiding duplication and missed deadlines.

- If you have recruited volunteers who want to learn more about office procedures, typing or computer skills, your secretary is the right role model and teacher.

- By supervising a volunteer corps, your secretary can develop and prove her/his abilities as a supervisor, which is often required for advancement into higher positions.

Remember to allow the secretary to determine the weekly schedule for volunteer clerical help, since s/he knows the flow of work (peak times, slow times) and when work space and equipment are available on any given day. In fairness to a secretary actively assisting you in such ways, adjustments should be made in her/his previously-assigned workload. If you expect the tasks described here to be done well, be prepared to advocate that a realistic amount of time be freed up.

Receptionists

The reality is that the person who first answers your organization's main telephone line can turn a potential volunteer on or off about getting involved. Therefore, it is imperative to inform such staff about the details of the volunteer program and how to handle various types of calls. Train everyone to take complete messages when you are out or unable to take a call immediately, obtaining information that will be helpful and time-saving. At the very least, receptionists (or any other staff members who might be answering your telephone) should project a positive and friendly attitude to volunteer program participants. Whether on the phone or in person, this "greeting" function is critical to creating the feeling of being welcome in the organization, both when volunteers first venture in and as they return time after time.

The increased use of automated voice mail systems raises special issues. Your challenge is to insure that callers trying to reach the volunteer office are directed properly and are made to feel valued. Test your system: how easy is it to make contact with you, and how does the process feel?

If your setting has a staffed reception area, you may also be able to get help with:

- Distributing recruitment materials and other volunteer program information.

- Making appointments for prospective volunteer interviews.

- Greeting applicants and requesting that they complete preliminary forms.

- Overseeing volunteer timesheets/sign-in logs.

In any case, it is well worth a little of your time to include reception staff as members of your team. In many organizations, they are often overlooked and excluded from program planning. By making them aware of what volunteers are doing and why they are important to the work of the organization, you are recognizing these fellow staff as important players. This will, in turn, make them more receptive to your requests for assistance.

Maintenance/Custodial Staff

It never hurts to have the janitor on your side! Volunteer programs tend to have group meetings and special events requiring furniture rearrangements, audio-visual set ups, clean-up and after-hours assistance. You will quickly learn that the maintenance staff welcomes a few words of explanation about the volunteer program in general and special projects in particular. Their willing cooperation can save you much aggravation and assure the success of events. The maintenance crew are experts in their area and may help you find previously unknown "gold mines" of stored furniture and supplies. Their skills in such things as carpentry can also come in very handy. If your maintenance staff deals with outside vendors, they may have valuable suggestions of possible donors for a great variety of needs and help you scrounge for materials.

Public Relations

If you work in a large organization, you may have access to staff in units tangential to yours. One prime example of this is Public Relations. Seek out their expertise as consultants and see if you can combine work. For example, the p.r. staff can design your information to coordinate with other agency materials. At the very least, a description of volunteer opportunities can be included in any overall agency brochures, displays, etc. They may also arrange media contacts, assist with press releases, and take photographs at volunteer events. Remind the p.r. staff that you help with their work, too, every time you go into the community and represent the organization.

Because of the natural similarities between the p.r. function and your outreach role as volunteer program coordinator, it is critical that the two complement each other and work together.

Consider the value of asking your administrator to require such cooperation from the beginning and to assist in clarifying decision-making authority, confirming that volunteer program projects accepted by the p.r. staff are not to be relegated to lowest priority. Determine the most effective communication channels. This is one area in which the team approach to implementing volunteer program management can yield tremendous results, benefitting the organization in terms of image, community support, and even financial resources.

One note of caution: if you ask for help, be sure to state clearly and exactly what you want and then stay involved. Too many directors of volunteers have abandoned their brochures to the p.r. department and then have regretted the results. Public relations staff know about design, graphics and writing—you know about volunteers!

Development/Fundraising/Special Events

Another related area is Resource Development, and your organization may have staff doing development, fundraising, or special events. All studies show a strong correlation between people who give time and people who give money. So shouldn't you and the fundraising staff coordinate your efforts and materials to reach both audiences? At the very least, make sure you are aware of each other's outreach activities so that you do not duplicate efforts. At best, find ways to carry each other's messages to as wide an audience as possible. Appeals for donations should include mention of volunteer opportunities; volunteer recruitment materials should include the option of financial support. An additional incentive for the development staff to support you is the fact that the value of volunteer service can be used as in-kind match for grant proposals.

Human Resources

Yet another function with close ties to yours is that of Human Resources or Personnel. In fact, in some organizations, the coordinator of volunteers is located within this unit. After all, the same principles apply to effective management of workers, whether those workers are employees or volunteers. So staff with human resource development expertise can be a valuable asset to you. They are a good source of information about interviewing techniques, personnel-related laws, risk management practices, policy development and screening procedures. They can also be alert to potential volunteers among job applicants, and actually refer prospects to you.

Another task they can assist with is volunteer orientation. Often there are standard materials (or even regularly-scheduled sessions) for new employees which can be adapted for use with new volunteers. In many organizations, it makes sense for the personnel staff to handle the screening of volunteers right along with that of employees, and to maintain certain records as well. They may be reluctant to assume these duties, especially if they view the volunteer program as "separate" or "different." This can be overcome if you include personnel staff in your planning and increase their awareness of exactly what the volunteers are doing.

Training is often a responsibility of human resources. One specific way in which this unit can support your team approach is to include information about the volunteer program in the orientation for all new salaried staff. This is an excellent way to ensure that everyone in the organization understands the role of volunteer resources in relation to the overall mission and goals, and to explain how everyone contributes. By stating the expectations and philosophy in the beginning, new staff are much more likely to be enthusiastic team members. Again, you may need to ask the top administrator to establish this policy, and suggest that either you or s/he participate in the orientation to carry the message.

Not all of us are skilled trainers, so you may feel this is one area that is much better delegated to those with this expertise. If in-service training is conducted for employees, perhaps volunteers can participate in these sessions as well—all of which are planned by someone other than you. Or, human resource staff may be able to identify specific trainers who can meet your needs and arrange for them to present sessions for volunteers.

Board of Directors

If you are with a nonprofit organization, your board members are, of course, volunteers—although you may be surprised to discover that some of them do not think of themselves as such. Or, even if they acknowledge their own voluntary status, they might draw a distinction between their policy-making function and the roles played by the "program" (direct service) volunteers. Legitimately, the primary concerns of the board relate to the overall functioning of the organization, of which volunteer involvement is only one component. However, it is important that board members understand that successful community volunteer involvement leads to positive public relations, expanded services, and even better fundraising.

The first thing the board needs to do to assist you is set policy regarding volunteers. This includes many of the issues already mentioned in Chapter 2. Members must make the commitment to support and encourage volunteer involvement—and you. On a continuous basis, board officers and members can assist with such tasks as:

- Distributing recruitment materials at their workplace and other gatherings they attend.

- Including mention of volunteer opportunities in any public speaking they do on behalf of the overall organization.

- Handling public speaking dates you may arrange specifically for volunteer recruitment.

- Participating in volunteer orientation and/or training sessions.

- Attending and helping with volunteer recognition events.

- Conducting volunteer program evaluation studies.

Admittedly, you may not have direct access to the board, especially in a large organization. If this is the case, you must work with your top administrator to insure that the board is knowledgeable about the volunteer component. One strategy may be to request that you attend at least one board meeting a year to make a presentation, answer questions, and enlist support. Another option is to ask the board to form a sub-committee on volunteer development. It could consist of several board members, a few direct service volunteers and yourself, and would provide a pool of people to rely on for a variety of delegated tasks. Such a committee also serves as a vehicle for keeping volunteer- related issues and information before the entire board. (See *The Board's Role in Effective Volunteer Involvement* by Susan J. Ellis, The National Center on Nonprofit Boards, 1995.)

Executive Director/Top Administrator

Several ways in which upper management can assist the volunteer program have already surfaced. It is especially appropriate for the executive to insure good employee/volunteer relations. There are three approaches top administrators can take. One is to issue mandates, requiring all staff to welcome partnership with volunteers. This may be appropriate (and necessary) in some cases, such as setting the policy that volunteer program information be included in orientation for all new staff. Another approach is to provide positive reinforcement for those staff who willingly join the volunteer management team on their own initiative. Finally, the director can lead by example and request volunteers to assist him or her directly. You and the executive should discuss the value of each of these approaches and make conscious decisions about when to utilize each. (Again, see *From the Top Down.*)

Just as already listed under the board of directors above, the executive should be willing to represent the volunteer program in the community. To demonstrate that volunteers are valued, the executive may even offer some clerical support from his/her own secretary, either on an on-going basis, or periodically to help with specific tasks such as preparing for volunteer training or recognition.

Program Staff

Program staff members who directly supervise volunteers on a day-to-day basis are already helping you a great deal. These supervisors are in reality adjunct volunteer program staff, as well as social workers, probation officers, park rangers, librarians, or whatever. Once they agree to work with volunteers, such staff have also accepted the responsibility to support and assist the entire program and you. You need to reach this understanding by continued dialogue.

Specific ways staff supervisors of volunteers can help manage the overall program are:

- Assessing the needs for volunteers within their area and clarifying assignments; writing volunteer job descriptions.

- Developing progressive assignments to challenge and "promote" experienced volunteers.

- Assisting with orientation of new volunteers.

- Designing and conducting initial training for volunteers assigned directly to them.

- Training other staff to be effective volunteer supervisors.

- Keeping volunteers motivated and recognized.

- Monitoring volunteer forms and reports; responding to concerns raised and informing you of possible problem areas before they get out of hand.

- Conducting individual volunteer performance assessments and assisting with program evaluation.

- Acting as recruiters and community resource developers, especially in tapping groups to which they belong professionally or personally.

- Sharing talents not necessarily job-related, such as doing art work for posters or providing entertainment at a special event.

- Sharing "success stories" with their co-workers at staff meetings, to highlight specific examples of how volunteers are contributing to the agency's goals.

Look around you. The first members of your management team are very near by.

5

FINDING YOUR MANAGEMENT TEAM: OUTSIDE

Having made full use of available in-house resources, you are now ready to tap the community for additional members of your management team. Your Task Analysis and identification of necessary skill areas point to a broad variety of team members waiting to be recruited.

Administrative Volunteers

"Administrative volunteers" are volunteers specifically recruited to help run the volunteer program. This is their only assignment. In addition to adding valuable time which you don't have, assigning volunteers to assist you directly has two other benefits: it demonstrates to the rest of staff that you, too, are willing to utilize volunteers in substantial ways; and it offers meaningful assignments to those volunteers preferring administrative rather than direct-service roles.

Be careful not to confuse administrative volunteers with clerical workers. Administrative volunteers are actually "assistant directors of volunteers," carrying major responsibility for key aspects of program coordination.

Select administrative volunteers on the basis of their special skills and as a complement to your own strengths and weaknesses. Trained administrative volunteers can often substitute for you in your absence, knowing enough about the overall operation of the program to act knowledgeably. They can also attend meetings on your behalf. Yes, it takes time to train a volunteer to be such an assistant, but the long-term pay-off is worth the effort.

Consider the following potential jobs that can be delegated to an administrative volunteer. Each can be a self-contained assignment, or one administrative volunteer can handle several, depending on his or her weekly schedule with you. As you read these suggestions, think about the kinds of skills and interests a volunteer would need to handle each function—you'll find your cadre of administrative assistants will be quite a diverse group of people!

Orientation Coordinator. Responsibilities include:
- designing a standardized orientation program
- scheduling sessions when needed
- lining up necessary speakers
- inviting new volunteers to attend
- assembling handout material
- chairing sessions
- conducting facility tours
- following up with those who do not come
- conducting special, adapted orientation sessions for groups or individuals

In-service Training Leader. Responsibilities include:
- identifying needed or desired topics/speakers
- scheduling training dates
- inviting speakers
- publicizing sessions
- coordinating refreshments, room arrangements, etc.
- chairing group meetings
- evaluating training

Shift Leader. Responsibilities include:
- providing on-site supervision and support for volunteer activities during a time period when you are not present, such as an evening or weekend day

52

– providing week-day coverage if you are on a part-time
work schedule

Researcher. Responsibilities include:
– conducting intensive studies on subjects requested by
you and/or the agency
– reviewing reference books and journals (this includes
keeping you informed about volunteerism resources)
– conducting written and oral surveys
– contacting outside sources of information
– ordering resource materials
– analyzing data and writing reports
– developing and managing an agency library

Resource Developer. Responsibilities include:
– "scrounging" materials and items needed by either the
volunteer program as a whole or by individual staff,
clients, or direct-service volunteers
– identifying necessary items and potential donors
– publicizing donation needs
– soliciting donors or resources
– keeping records of all contacts and results
– thanking resources utilized and giving them public
credit as appropriate
– letting volunteers and salaried staff know of items available

Newsletter Editor. Responsibilities include:
– producing a regularly-published volunteer newsletter
or other in-house forms of written communication
– soliciting articles
– interviewing key people
– gathering announcement data
– maintaining distribution lists
– supervising layout
– selecting art work and making design decisions

Project Coordinator. This administrative volunteer supervises a
cluster of volunteers involved in a project not directly
under the jurisdiction of a salaried staff member. Such
projects may be experimental or may provide an extra

service—anything that would fall to you to supervise if you did not have an administrative volunteer to handle it. As "project coordinator," a volunteer should have the responsibility inherent in the title, including:

- some recruiting and screening of other volunteers for the project
- training and supervising project workers
- keeping records on project progress

In essence, the project coordinator keeps the project going, with you providing periodic support and guidance.

Records Manager. Responsibilities include:
- conducting research to determine what kind of information you need to be collecting
- developing whatever paper or computerized system you need to track volunteer involvement
- designing forms and training staff and volunteers on how to use them
- entering information from volunteer timesheets
- producing periodic reports summarizing activities and impact
- searching for donated computer equipment
- adapting software and training staff on how to use it

Troubleshooter. Responsibilities include:
- keeping in touch with volunteers and salaried staff on a periodic, informal basis to assure that everything is going smoothly
- providing volunteers an extra "ear" as a sort of ombudsman service
- helping volunteers who work off-site to maintain a strong connection to the organization

(This role requires a special, diplomatic individual who will be sensitive to issues which may arise involving volunteer/staff relationships.)

Surrogate. Responsibilities include:
- representing you at community gatherings such as tours
  of new community agencies, government hearings, conferences or meetings with key sources of volunteers
  (i.e., church board meetings, college field placement
  program meetings)
- participating in staff meetings when you cannot be
  present, to share information about volunteer activities

Whatever their specific assignment area, administrative
volunteers should be trained to think with you about the volunteer
program as a whole. On the next page is a list of tips for administrative volunteers, offered as a useful training tool to help articu-
late the unique aspects of this role.

Recruiting administrative volunteers

Occasionally, directors of volunteers express reluctance
about seeking administrative volunteers out of a sense of obligation to give priority to organizational needs other than their own.
It feels like "skimming from the top" to divert skilled people from
other volunteer positions. Look at this another way: It makes
good sense to involve high quality volunteers on behalf of the volunteer program because this, in turn, provides a stronger degree of
support to all volunteers who follow.

Another concern is that prospective volunteers who
inquire about direct service work are really not interested in a role
in program administration. This is often true. Therefore, you cannot be passive about hoping that a good administrative candidate
will be discovered through your regular volunteer recruiting. If
you sincerely want this type of help, you must actively recruit for
it. Most people are unaware that the opportunity exists to help
manage a volunteer program because most recruitment campaigns
discuss only assignments related to the direct service areas of the
organization. Yet there are people for whom the challenge and
scope of this type of leadership role is truly appealing.

Here are some tips for recruiting administrative volunteers:

- Remember that if you are enthusiastic about your role,
  others can be, too. Sell the assignment based on what
  you enjoy most about the job—variety, people contact,
  creativity, management experience, etc.

Tips for Administrative Volunteers

- Stay **well informed** about as many different aspects of the volunteer program as possible. This includes both "big picture" and nitty-gritty details. You will be expected to be able to answer questions from both employees and volunteers, and it is critical that you provide accurate responses.

- **Details** do matter! When beginning a large project, conduct a mental "walk through" to identify weaknesses in the plan. By thinking about what could go wrong, you can build in safeguards and additional procedures to minimize the chance of error or disaster. (This is risk management at its best!)

- Learn to be an **active listener**. Part of your role is to help identify needs that are going unmet, gaps in existing services, or problems that are beginning to emerge. Tune in to what is going on around you and share the concerns you are hearing with your supervisor (or the director of volunteers) in order to help him/her plan ahead and remain proactive.

- Similarly, remember your responsibility to help **convey information** from the management team to direct service volunteers and line staff. This may include interpreting policies, explaining the what and why of procedures, and offering information about changes which are occurring in the organization.

- Be mindful of the fact that you may be perceived as walking a fine line between paid staff and volunteers. If you were formerly a direct-service volunteer, do you now identify with "Management" or "Program"? Has the nature of your relationship with other volunteers changed? How do employees regard your function? The trick is to **maintain a balance**, ideally with credibility in both worlds, so you can effectively help move the organization forward.

- If you encounter **resistance** to some program need from either salaried staff or volunteers, diagnose the cause: differing priorities? lack of information about you? lack of information about them? bad timing? pre-conceived assumptions? Once you have identified the reason for resistance it is much easier to deal with it constructively.

- As a member of the management team, one of your most important tasks is to help set the tone for effective volunteer involvement in the organization. This can be accomplished in many ways: common courtesy to everyone; on-going acknowledgment of each person's contributions; encouraging teamwork; a sincere and honest approach to problem-solving; demonstrating daily that you "walk the talk." The combined effect of these types of behavior will be a **climate** that is welcoming, productive, and sustainable.

- Remember that the skills you are developing and/or using as a member of the management team are transferable to other jobs and other settings. Be alert to the **learning opportunities** around you. If you plan to use this as work experience on a resume, keep a log of specific responsibilities and activities you manage.

- **Enjoy yourself!** Volunteer management is exciting, fun and full of unexpected rewards.

- Write a specific job description, just as you would for any other volunteer position. Include definitive areas of responsibility, showing what you plan to delegate. (Use the list above as a starting point.) Do not simply say you need someone to "assist the Director of Volunteers." Your job is too large and complex (and mysterious!) to assume someone understands what assisting you means, so identify a specific cluster of tasks which clarify what the volunteer will do. As illustrated above, use titles that reflect each person's role, rather than using "Administrative Volunteer" as everyone's title.

- Be honest about the necessary time commitment. For an administrative volunteer to both handle some specific area of responsibility and stay informed about overall volunteer program activities, s/he probably needs to be on duty at least two days a week. If you are only in the office a few days a week yourself, you may want to find someone who can cover the volunteer program on the days you are absent. This should be clearly explained in the job description, along with a plan for overlapping some time for supervision and reporting.

- On the other hand, one of the advantages to some of the administrative functions previously described is that they can be done with an irregular schedule (weekends, evenings, odd hours) or even outside the office or at home. Volunteers who find this flexibility attractive can therefore handle projects or product-oriented assignments, rather than those that involve regular, on-site substitution for you.

Where can you look for potential administrative volunteers?

Some people have been leaders for years in countless organizations but have never stopped to consider that they could contribute to the *management* of an agency volunteer program. Seek out the past presidents of all-volunteer groups, pointing out that being an officer in a club or association is excellent training in volunteer administration. Such proven leaders are a good source of potential administrative volunteers for you, and may enjoy this new application of their skills.

Another good source is students. The current emphasis on youth community service and service-learning means that more and more students (high school, college, and graduate) are looking for opportunities to volunteer in public and nonprofit organizations. Some will be intrigued by the role of administrative volunteer. They will recognize the immense learning possibilities of working with a manager such as yourself, and generally like the variety of an assignment that provides broader exposure to the entire organization.

Consider describing some of these positions as "internships in volunteer administration." It may be a motivating factor to point out that volunteer administration is a growing career field and that administrative volunteers can learn skills and demonstrate abilities that may later lead to job opportunities in a variety of settings. This is particularly appealing to students, homemakers, or career switchers wanting to put administrative experience on their résumé to enhance their chances for employment.

Several of the task areas are very well suited to student skills. Be open to creating assignments to match academic majors. For instance, a journalism major may be delighted to design and conduct a mass media publicity/recruitment campaign for you, while a social work candidate might prefer assisting with volunteer supervision and follow-up. Geography students may be interested in working on a demographic study of your city to help locate sites for special targeted recruitment efforts. Today's students are seeking practical experience in every conceivable field, so the options are endless.

Certain administrative volunteer jobs require advanced professional skills, so start by brainstorming who has those skills. This may lead you to professional societies, special interest associations, and other places where you can express your need for help to an audience with the expertise you seek. While some people may prefer volunteering to be a change of pace from their paid work life, others are pleased to be able to apply their knowledge to a different setting.

Because you probably only need one or two people in each skill area, if you target your recruitment to the right audience, you have an excellent chance of success.

Advisors

Regardless of whether or not your organization has an established board of directors or community advisory council, you might consider developing a group of advisors specifically for you and the volunteer program. Such advisors can act as a sounding board for new ideas and as a source of suggestions and problem-solving help. Their primary purpose is to be a "think tank." Advisors do not necessarily have to help with day-to-day project implementation, though they need to be kept informed of the program's status. You can select individuals to be advisors for three reasons:

- they represent program participants (volunteers, salaried staff, board members);
- they represent recipients of service (consumers, clients, or general public);
- they have expertise or a skill you need (financial management, legal knowledge, public relations contacts).

You can either work with advisors individually or as a group. If you decide to form an "advisory committee," be sure you have a clear purpose for doing so. What is accomplished by a committee that cannot be done one-to-one or in small clusters? There may be something gained from large group interaction, but only if everyone participates fully and the task is clear. Do not assume that it saves time to hold a few group meetings as opposed to several individual contacts. It may be more productive and less time-consuming to work one-on-one. It depends on what kind of help you need, and when.

The best approach may be a mixture: informing advisors (when you recruit them) that they might be invited to a general meeting and may be asked for shorter, personal consultations on an as-needed basis. This flexibility lets you get the maximum from each and every volunteer. You can then title such volunteers as "program advisors" rather than as "members of the advisory group." This places more responsibility on each person, instead of shifting it onto a group that then has to be managed.

When you seek out advisors to act as consultants, it is important to specify whether you want them to *do* or to *advise*, and the exact tasks with which you expect to need their assistance. For example, you might ask a local radio station manager to review your public service announcements in draft form for a year. During that time you would probably fax or e-mail him or her your public service message ideas and request editorial remarks. Once or twice you might ask for a brief meeting (at the radio station, for his/her convenience) so that you can discuss your overall media strategy and receive general advice. At the end of a year, using this approach, you will have received valuable help and the radio station manager will have been utilized in the most suitable—and time-efficient—manner.

Most people are flattered to be regarded as expert advisors, and will agree to help if they trust you to stick with your promise of only calling on them when their particular skill is needed. Avoid recruiting advisors for "political" reasons. Yes, it might be lovely to have a V.I.P.'s spouse on your list of advisors. But if s/he has no relevant managerial skill to offer, why add a token member to your team who will be a further drain on your precious time?

Modern technology now provides access to advisors well beyond the boundaries of your own community. Through e-mail and special computer bulletin boards and newsgroups, you can tap the expertise of specialists anywhere in the world. People have already demonstrated willingness to be helpful in answering questions posed in cyberspace. Indications are that this type of technical assistance volunteering will become more organized and accessible through organizations now being formed for this purpose.

Organized Groups

There are countless civic, social, religious, business, professional, and fraternal clubs and associations in every community which you may already be approaching on behalf of the volunteer program. But if your "pitch" is focused only on recruiting their members as individuals, you are missing the chance to get an additional type of help. Beyond giving donations of money and things, and beyond sponsoring one-shot special events, groups can handle certain aspects of your program on an ongoing basis.

How about asking a group to "adopt" an area of responsibility for a year or more? Or adopt a day of the week to staff the children's play room or the gift shop? Or plan and implement all holiday activities? This means that group leaders commit to coordinating their members in accomplishing necessary tasks in these function areas. These leaders—not you—recruit workers, orient them, train them, supervise them, and keep records. You work with the leaders only, though periodically you might meet with everyone involved.

Ideas for ongoing projects that can be delegated to an outside group for independent management include: gift shops, shopping assistance services; transportation programs; repair of donated items; renovation projects; tutoring for special clients; sports programs; and client outings.

Although a group agrees to handle a major service area and will save you the day-to-day management tasks, you are still responsible for some of the basics, such as:

- Determining and interpreting your organization's policies and procedures.
- Developing a standardized recordkeeping system.
- Assuring the quality and standards of volunteer service.
- Providing screening criteria, job descriptions, training designs and procedures.
- Reviewing periodic reports and being accessible to group leaders for questions and problem-solving.
- Planning ways to recognize the group's work and say thank you to its members.

Corporations/Businesses

Volunteering by corporate employees is a source of help for nonprofit and public organizations. Not just confined to large, national corporations, many smaller, local firms and businesses are encouraging their employees to become actively involved in some form of community service. In some cases, a company simply keeps its personnel aware of volunteer opportunities and workers volunteer on their own time. In other models, employees who volunteer are actually given some "work release time" away from their jobs. Some firms even have an in-house Employee Volunteer Program Coordinator who serves as a liaison with community groups requesting help.

In terms of being a resource for your management team, corporations can be tapped in two ways: as a self-organized group of volunteers, or as a pool of specific expertise.

If you have a special project that needs to be handled on an organized basis, you could approach a company with the idea of "sponsoring" it. Once interested employees are identified, your relationship with them will follow the model of any other organized group, as discussed above. The only real difference is that this corporate group may not have a structure already in place (such as officers) to take over the administrative/coordinating functions of the project. So it might be part of your initial training to establish a workable plan for on-going management. Your goal, after all, is to create a *self-supervising* group.

Apart from this type of regularly-scheduled help, corporations can serve as a "skills bank" to meet your periodic needs for advice and technical assistance. Examples of things with which you might appropriately ask for help include:

- Recruitment materials: graphic design of brochures and other publicity items; art work; writing copy; specs for printing; selection of paper, color and format.

- Financial systems: budget development; bookkeeping procedures; accountability methods; best utilization of computers.

- Training for you: consultation in management, public relations, supervision, staff relations, delegation, time management, report writing, planning and evaluation. Another option would be to allow you or a team member to sit in on employee training sessions on such subjects.

- Training for volunteers: expert speakers for in-service training on topics such as interviewing, time management, conflict resolution and legal issues.

Collaborations

Despite much lip service about mutual goals and shared community concerns, it is still rare to find concrete examples of actual collaboration among agencies and associations. In fact, when it comes to recruiting and retaining volunteers, groups are often competitive rather than cooperative. Yet jointly-sponsored projects can be exciting and beneficial to all participants—as well as time-saving for you.

There are two logical ways to identify possible partners for volunteer program collaboration. You can either approach several organizations having a similar purpose or client group (e.g., all youth-serving agencies, all cultural groups, all crime prevention programs), or you can invite all organizations that are your "neighbors" within a geographical area (e.g., ten city blocks or one rural square mile). Don't be limited by town boundaries and county lines; think about what organizations surround you, regardless of mailing address.

A "Collaboration Grid" worksheet to stimulate your thinking about collaborative partners is shown on the next page. The goal is to identify community entities with which you share some common denominator, though you may otherwise be very different. Rather than gravitating towards organizations similar to yours (with the danger of feeling competitive), this Grid will expand your horizons about possible collaborative resources. For example, on the surface it might seem as if the senior center and the elementary after-school program have little in common until you realize that both focus their programming during late afternoon hours. This fact could be the starting point for a shared transportation system, an intergenerational project, etc.

Instructions for using the Grid are:

1. First, complete the left-hand column.

    a. Under "Client/Consumer Group," identify your organization's client group(s). Do you serve children? seniors? families? Spanish-speaking people? persons with physical disabilities?

    b. Next identify the "Type of Service" you offer: counseling, vocational training, historical preservation, etc.

    c. Then move to "Geographic Area" and any "Special Focus."

    Since the object of this worksheet is to be as specific as possible, if your organization has multiple client groups, services or sites, you should consider using several grids to focus on each.

Collaboration Grid

	Organizations Sharing this Focus	Businesses Sharing this Focus	Individuals & Other Linkages Sharing this Focus
Our Organization			
Our Client/Consumer Group:			
Our Type of Service:			
Our Geographic Area:			
Other Special Focus:			

2. Now work across each row to determine who else shares the same focus. For example, if you serve children, the "Organizations" square might list "schools," "Scouts," etc.. Be sure to include both nonprofit and public entities, large and small. The "Businesses" square might include "toy stores," "music stores," "kids' clothing stores," etc. The "Other Linkages" square might list "Mayor's Commission on Youth," "child psychologists," "music teachers," etc.

It is very likely that some of the organizations you identify through the Collaboration Grid also have volunteer components. Chances are that the other directors of volunteers you uncover are as overworked and under-assisted as you are! Therefore, they may welcome the chance to work with you in a variety of ways.

In some communities there may already be a "DOVIA" group. This is the generic term for "Directors of Volunteers in Agencies," though your local group may have a different name. DOVIA meetings provide members with mutual support, idea exchange, and fertile ground for developing collaborative relationships. The following ideas explore the potential for significant teamwork among volunteer programs:

Resource sharing:

Make an inventory of the assets and needs of each organization, including meeting space, special equipment, training materials, and volunteers/employees with unusual expertise (artists, foreign language speakers, sign language interpreters). If each group agrees to exchange something during the course of a month or even a year, you have all multiplied your resources.

Volunteer recruitment:

Believe it or not, several organizations can recruit at the same time and the same place without being in competition! Each organization has different assignments and schedules available which appeal to various ages, personalities, and levels of skill— even if, at first glance, you are all helping children, the arts, whatever. Your differences are actually more apparent when you recruit together than alone. Specific joint recruitment ideas include:

65

– Run cooperative newspaper ads.
– Propose to the local media that they do a feature story on each of you, either in a series or all at once.
– Design one large display incorporating everyone's materials and schedule it at various public places and events. You can then rotate responsibility for staffing the display, which means your program gets publicized in perhaps ten places, but you only spend time yourself in one.

In-service training:

If your collaborative partners share a common service focus you can develop a "training cooperative." Simply put, together you develop a list of useful topics that would benefit everyone's volunteers; then you plan a year-long schedule of sessions, usually on the same day each month. Each member of the "training cooperative" agrees to run one or two sessions during the year. All volunteers in each organization in the cooperative are invited to all sessions, but you are only responsible for planning and implementing one or two actual sessions.

The benefits of such a plan are enormous. Your volunteers get twelve excellent programs and the chance to mingle with other volunteers who share a mutual interest, whether it's working with teenagers or advocacy skills. Sites can be rotated, providing the added feature of a new facility tour each time. Most of the year you have nothing to do. When your turn to run the program comes around, you can concentrate on making it especially successful, rather than dissipating your energies in planning many sessions by yourself (which may not even attract a good turnout). And remember, you can always find an administrative volunteer to handle your assigned session(s)!

Volunteer newsletter content:

Many organizations have volunteer newsletters which also fulfill an in-service training function. Why should every organization write its own tips on listening skills, updates on legislation, etc., when this work could be shared? Like the training cooperative just described, several groups could select subjects of mutual interest and agree upon submission deadlines. Each group then accepts responsibility, on a rotating basis, for writing either a column or an insert to be used in everyone's newsletter. It is also possible to recruit volunteers to research issues pertinent to all of you, such as legislation, books and resources, or local controversies, and to report these for joint use in everyone's newsletters.

Volunteer recognition:

Instead of everyone pursuing recognition gifts, meals, and certificates individually, you might try co-sponsoring one big event. This way you can coordinate and share the work of appeals to donors. You can divide up major tasks such as refreshments and entertainment. You may discover that a number of people are actually volunteers in several of the cooperating programs, and so a shared event can add to the impact and quality of recognizing these active citizens. Collaborative recognition makes the event a real community function. It also provides a level of visibility that no one organization could achieve on its own.

Even if everyone does their own in-house recognition event, you may still want to collaborate on a community-wide celebration of National Volunteer Week.

Volunteer transportation:

In an era of environmentalism, reduced (or non-existent) mass transit systems and increased crime, many organizations find transportation to be the biggest recruitment and retention roadblock (pun intended!). For organizations especially interested in recruiting young students, low-income community service workers, or senior citizens, transportation will be a shared priority. This situation is an opportunity for collaboration on car pools and other alternative transportation systems. Volunteers from several organizations can also study area transportation needs and formulate recommendations, urging lawmakers to provide better services. Volunteers can even raise funds to purchase vans for joint transportation arrangements, or seek donations of vehicles.

Child care and other support:

Lack of child care is often a barrier preventing low-income adults and single parents from becoming active volunteers. Why not collaborate on a child care service for use by volunteers while on the job? One idea is small babysitting cooperatives among groups of volunteers. Another, especially if you are co-located with several agencies in one building or area, is to set aside child care space and jointly recruit volunteers or paid staff to provide supervision. "Enabling funds" to reimburse volunteers for child care and other out-of-pocket expenses are often hard to include in an agency budget. But what about a community-wide fundraising event specifically for such costs? The resulting funds could then be managed by a volunteer board or council representing the organizations that helped to raise the money.

You may have some reservations about your ability to manage these types of collaborative efforts. Define each partner's role, develop systems of communication, and keep things as simple as possible. Note that the number of participating organizations will affect the type of projects you can undertake. Too many—more than ten, in fact—is probably unwieldy for decision making and for holding everyone accountable for doing their share.

You may also have legitimate concerns that organizational jurisdictions and policies will interfere with the success of collaboration efforts. If your community has an inter-agency council that is already coordinating programs and services, start with those agencies. It is likely that the subject of volunteers has not yet been placed on the agenda, but there is a foundation of trust on which to build.

On the other hand, you may be proposing joint projects among agencies and groups that ordinarily have no formalties or may even be officially restricted from contact (such as being from two counties). But one of the wonderful things about volunteers is that, as private citizens, they are not bound by such artificial limits. You can overcome bureaucratic technicalities by encouraging each interested group to appoint a volunteer representative to something like a "Volunteerism Collaboration Council." Such a council can explore the potential for implementing joint projects and act as a catalyst for new levels of cooperation, with liaison support from you and your staff counterparts. Encourage the group to start with simple, small steps to build trust, and then sit back and enjoy the results!

Recruiting management team members from outside the organization requires you to be a community organizer. The more bridges you build, the stronger your team and the whole volunteer program.

6

IMAGINE THIS

To help you visualize the possibilities of the team approach to volunteer management, here are a number of scenarios that demonstrate its application to a variety of situations. Read these to spark your creative thinking about how you might recruit helpers in your setting.

Chapters 7 and 8 will return to more practical how-to's of making a team management system work.

Scenario 1: The Branch Librarian

    I am the primary professional in my branch library and depend on a small core of paid staff and volunteers to deliver services to our library users. Recently the central library administration has initiated a community-wide campaign to encourage more people to support their library. So I've been getting calls from area residents who want to volunteer...and all the publicity has attracted some new customers, too.
I'VE JUST READ THIS BOOK!
    Now I have a few ideas for how I might develop a volunteer program management team that expands our services without requiring a whole lot more of my time:

    ■ *We could set aside a "Homework Corner" for school children who need a place to study between 3:00 p.m. and closing. I'll find a volunteer to be Homework Corner Coordinator to talk with the kids to find out what they really need in the way of help. The Coordinator can then develop volunteer job descriptions and procedures for how this Corner will operate. I can direct some of the calls from people interested in volunteering to the Coordinator, because it shouldn't take too much training in library skills for someone to help in this new service.*

    ■ *It seems as if a lot of the new customers are Korean and in English-language classes. If I could recruit a volunteer bilingual in Korean and English, it would be much easier to serve these new residents. This New Citizens Mentor can translate some of our basic instruction sheets for using the library, interpret by phone if necessary, survey this population for their book needs, and host welcome orientations. The Mentor could work pretty independently and check in with me as necessary.*

    ■ *My busiest day is Friday. And it always seems as if the most volunteers want to come in that day, too. I think I'll* ask one of our long-term experienced volunteers to become the Friday Shift Leader to take the pressure off of me for at least a few hours on that day.

Scenario 2: The Executive Director

I am the executive of a small nonprofit agency having five paid staff (not all full-time), an active board of directors, and a few direct service volunteers who have been with us since we opened our doors three years ago. The demand for our services is skyrocketing. We are fundraising for expansion, but know we have to increase the number of volunteers, too. No one on staff has any training in working with volunteers.

I'VE JUST READ THIS BOOK!

Now I have a few ideas for how I might develop a volunteer program management team that expands our services without eating up all my time:

- I'm going to ask my paid administrative assistant to read this book, too. Then I'll talk with her about doing some things that will start to structure how we manage volunteer involvement, such as developing job descriptions, better recordkeeping forms, an orientation and training plan. I'm also going to buy a volunteer records software package and require our part-time bookkeeper to learn how to use it, enter all current volunteers, and keep up with new data monthly.

- I'll ask the board to form a Volunteer Expansion Task Force. Once we have job descriptions, this Task Force can help me to recruit some new skilled volunteers. Also, I want this group to identify some specific ways we can creatively recognize and thank our volunteers throughout the year. (We've been doing a pretty bad job at this so far, and I've felt so guilty about it!)

71

■ *Maybe I'll contact our local DOVIA and use my powers of persuasion to find a professional director of volunteers who would agree to be an advisor to me for six months as we formalize and expand our volunteer efforts. I think I'll use the approach of "this will be great career development in learning how to consult." Also, maybe I could offer—in exchange—to be that person's advisor on some "executive" subject like board development or understanding financial statements.*

Scenario 3: The Activities Director

I am the Activities Director in a medium-sized, long-term care facility. My degree is in occupational therapy but here I juggle many roles, including recreational services, religious programs, holiday events, and some public relations. Volunteers are also expected to report to me. I really like volunteers, but never have much time to focus on them. I never actively recruit; people call on their own if they're interested. I used to get a lot of older volunteers from church groups who liked the few assignments available. Now I'm getting calls from a lot of students and they seem to want more challenging things to do. Meanwhile, we seem to be accepting more bed-bound residents who need individualized help.

I'VE JUST READ THIS BOOK!

Now I have a few ideas for how I might develop a volunteer program management team that will help coordinate all the demands on me:

■ *I need an administrative volunteer for each of the job responsibility areas I have, other than occupational therapy (though maybe later I can use help there, too). If I can find four people with the skills to be Recreation Coordinator, Chaplaincy Liaison, Holiday Planner, and Public Relations Assistant, just think of how much I could*

72

delegate to them. The Recreation Coordinator would probably need to have at least six hours a week to give me, but the other roles could be more flexible. Some of the work could even be done off-site. And the Holiday Planner could be taught to work with a different community organization "sponsor" for each major holiday. I'm sure that each of these folks could come up with volunteer job descriptions in their areas which would appeal to those students who keep calling.

Scenario 4: The Park Ranger

I am a parks and forestry management professional. I am the only full-time paid worker at my county park, with seasonal hourly employees in the summer. The county commissioners want to show tax payers that the park is continuing to serve residents even though our budget has not been increased in two years. Five years ago we formed a "Friends of the County Park" group and it is comprised of about twenty devoted supporters who have completed several small improvement projects. And the Girl and Boy Scouts really help every year with clean-up. I know we could do more with volunteers...but who has the time?

I'VE JUST READ THIS BOOK!

Now I have a few ideas for how I might develop a volunteer program management team that lets me respond to our needs without driving me crazy:

■ I'm going to call Joe, who I know just retired from the state department of environmental services and might be convinced to use his skills in a new way. He'd be great as a consultant to help me plan a more structured volunteer program here. I'll ask him to volunteer for one year in that capacity. He could do some research on model programs, draw up some job descriptions, and lead us to other resources at the state and local level. If he says no, maybe

I could get him to help find someone else.

■ *After we've done some initial thinking and are clearer on what we want, I'll ask the Friends to form a speakers bureau to help me generate community support for the park and recruit new direct service volunteers.*

■ *Because I work all weekends, I really worry about the park on Tuesdays, my day off. Even though it's a lot quieter here then and there's an employee in the office, there have been times when visitors have needed more help. I think I'll recruit a Tuesday Manager who would be out on the grounds, visible to the public. Because some days would be slow, this person might also do some hands-on work like maintaining the wild-flower garden.*

Scenario 5: The Full-time Director of Volunteers

I am the director of volunteers in an urban hospital. We have 300 volunteers each month and my paid staff includes a full-time secretary, youth volunteer director, and gift shop manager. Also, I have good cooperation from the Public Relations department which produces beautiful volunteer posters and brochures for me. Other departments do their bit, too. But health care is changing and the hospital is looking for new patient services. We've started a wellness program, stop-smoking clinic, mobile immunization unit, and are planning a new walk-in clinic in another part of town. And yesterday, the Director of Patient Services asked me to consider involving volunteers in follow-up calls to patients released early from the hospital. The volunteers I already have don't want to do these new things.

I'VE JUST READ THIS BOOK!

Now I have a few ideas for how I might add new components to my existing volunteer program management team to expand our services without adding more staff right now:

74

■ *I need help in becoming acquainted with the neighborhood around the new clinic site, and I'll also need help in supervising volunteers there when it opens. Maybe an administrative volunteer to be the "Clinic Volunteer Coordinator" is the answer. In the beginning, the medical staff will be too busy to give volunteers the right attention as everyone learns the ropes. Later, I'll work with the clinic director there to turn over volunteer supervision as in other hospital units. I'll try to recruit this Coordinator now through the tenant organization that is active in the neighborhood.*

■ *I'll bet several hospitals are also starting to do patient follow up. I'm going to call my colleagues and suggest that we form a Training Cooperative to teach volunteers how to make supportive telephone calls and to train them in the basic information they need in order to respond to questions and situations. Since this a new area for all of us, we can learn together what will work best—without having to duplicate efforts.*

■ *All these new assignment areas are going to require that I attract some new types of volunteers and so I'll have to change my recruiting habits. Truth to tell, I haven't really done much recruiting in recent years because enough people just find me. But those people aren't right for the new jobs. I need a Recruitment Specialist. Maybe a graduate student in marketing might be intrigued at this challenge. Together we could develop a recruitment strat-egy and the Recruitment Specialist could identify target audiences, write recruitment "pitches," and work with media. That would be wonderful!*

7

STRUCTURING YOUR TEAM

It seems fair to assume that you have achieved your position as volunteer administrator because of your skills in working with people. Though there is always room for refinement of technique, the basics of delegation, training, supervision, and motivation are skill areas you already use daily with all volunteers. In fact, *the major premise of bringing volunteers into an organization is to delegate tasks.* Just as you have to help others on staff learn how to share their jobs with volunteers, you yourself need to be comfortable with dividing up your responsibilities among members of your team.

Once again, keep in mind that the volunteer program is not "yours." If a possessive pronoun is needed at all, the more appropriate one is "their" program (the volunteers') or, better still, "our" program. This thinking will make it easier to delegate tasks as important program functions, rather than simply as pieces of your job. Encourage the perspective of "we're all in this together," instead of "you all have to help me get this done." This philosophy of leadership makes team management a logical way to operate.

77

Having reviewed the resources available for staffing the volunteer program management team, you are now ready to get people started, keep them going, and coordinate all this assistance effectively.

Delegation

Since delegation is such a critical part of this entire process, it seems pertinent to review its basic elements. There are numerous management textbooks that address the fine art of delegation, usually along with a discussion of such issues as authority, control, and willingness to share power. As stated above, your approach to delegation is not "how do I get people to do this?" but rather "what is the best way to share these tasks so that the entire organization can reap maximum benefits?" Within this conceptual framework, here are some guidelines to insure successful delegation:

- Select the most appropriate person to handle the task. Don't fall into the trap of settling for the nearest available warm body. Consider such criteria as the person's schedule, skills, work style and preferences.

- Formulate written job descriptions or assignment descriptions, tailored to the particular person if necessary. Do this for in-house employees as well as for volunteers, especially if the delegated work is not already covered in regular employee job descriptions. (Your ultimate goal may be to have appropriate volunteer-related activities integrated into employee job expectations.) Don't overlook the need to pin things down in writing when a committee or organized group is the "doer."

- Tasks you assign to others should be concrete and manageable, with clearly-defined timeframes and deadlines. Define complex tasks in stages, so that people can feel a sense of achievement as each benchmark is reached.

- Tell the truth about the time required to do the job properly and your expectations for when it should be finished. Similarly, whenever possible, assign the whole task at once, rather than revealing something new each week.

- Give people titles to match the responsibility they will be handling, and then consistently refer to these titles yourself.

- Give the person/group information that sets the task into context. People work more intelligently when they understand how their activities mesh with the activities of others, or how a present task builds on a previous one and, in turn, brings the organization closer to its goals.

- Identify resources and materials the person/group can use to get the job done.

- Never underestimate the importance of good instructions. A basic part of training, instructions are the key to starting a job. Do not assume that anyone, particularly a volunteer, is completely familiar with your office procedures, policies, legal regulations, or anything else affecting a task. Instructions can include samples of similar work; knowing how something was done in the past is a great beginning point for a new job.

- Discuss some alternate contingency plans, should an original tactic not be successful.

- Set limits: at what point must you be consulted or involved, approve expenditures, receive progress reports?

- Remove limits: encourage people to exercise creativity and initiative in those areas where there are no hard and fast rules to be followed, or where you feel they have adequate expertise.

- Develop a reporting plan: how often and in what form (meetings, written reports, audiotapes) will you communicate with each other about progress? Negotiate the frequency of contact necessary to offer mutual feedback and support.

- Once you've delegated, don't undercut the independence of the team member. For example, refer all questions about the delegated project to the person responsible.

- Make it a condition of starting a task that the person commit to training his/her successor or replacement. Though this may not always work perfectly because of the frequent time lag between needing a volunteer and finding one, people should know they are expected to help assure a project's continuity. Therefore they might even return to your organization for a day or two to help train the new team member. Another strategy is to ask team members to keep a written record of their procedures that can be passed on to their successors. None of us wants to think our hard work will be lost indefinitely, so passing the torch is satisfying.

When you first begin a new delegation, be sure you set a time to meet or talk again fairly soon. This appointment provides an incentive to the team member to make some progress by then and gives you the opportunity to assure yourself that things are off to a good start.

Coordinating Structures

Coordination is crucial to the success of your management team, since you will be working with several groups of people and with several people as individuals—all in your already limited time. One approach is to develop a team that operates as a managing body. It holds regular meetings at which decisions are made, much like a presidential cabinet. Each team member is responsible for a working component of the program and comes to team meetings ready to report on that component's progress, to request input, etc. As a group, the team discusses issues affecting the entire program and decides on the best way to handle activities. You are the team leader, though your opinion may or may not carry extra weight with the group. Note that this team is far from an "advisory" body—it is a working group with power to set priorities and make decisions.

A different approach to forming a team is to deal with each member individually, as a "department head." Though you may occasionally want to call a group meeting, business is conducted largely through regularly-scheduled meetings between you and each team member. As with the first option, team members are not simply advisors; they are in charge of program functions and report to you.

Obviously, there is room for a combination of management styles. Realistically, you might cluster several related team members into a decision-making group, while meeting individually with people who are handling tasks unrelated to the issues confronting the group team.

For your own sake and so that everyone understands where each team member fits in, it is important to illustrate your team graphically on paper. There are several ways this can be done. The diagram on the next page shows how the program is organized and how the structure places demands on you, as leader. It also demonstrates the "ripple effect" of how the management team in turn connects with many more workers, both paid and volunteer.

Another option is to develop an organizational chart clarifying the interrelationship of the volunteer program with the entire agency. First consider direct lines of supervision. In the example on page 83, note how the chart depicts the volunteers who are directly assigned to work with you and those being supervised by other employees in their own departments.

This same chart can be used to illustrate your volunteer management team. Add dotted lines to show who communicates and collaborates with each other in taking charge of the volunteer program, regardless of daily "placement" on the chart. Note there are also dotted lines among various volunteers who must coordinate with each other within units.

Division of Work

Another useful coordination tool is an Assignment Grid, on which you can plot the potential division of work among team members. An example is on pages 86-87. First list the tasks to be

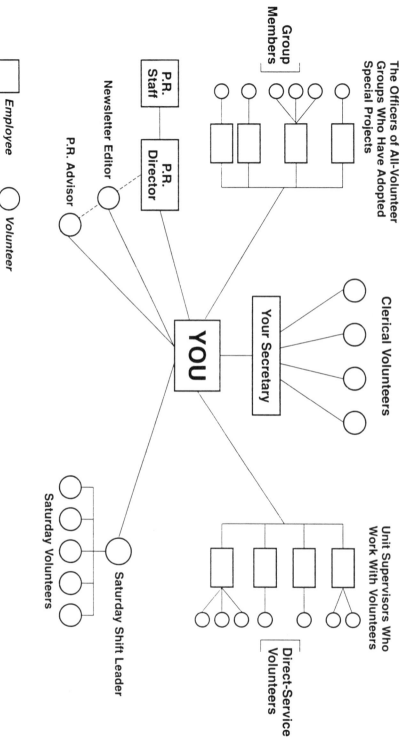

Volunteer Management Team Diagram

The Officers of All-Volunteer
Groups Who Have Adopted
Special Projects

Group
Members

Employee

Volunteer

P.R.
Staff

Newsletter Editor

P.R.
Director

P.R. Advisor

YOU

Your Secretary

Clerical Volunteers

Saturday
Saturday Volunteers

Saturday Shift Leader

Unit Supervisors Who
Work With Volunteers

Direct-Service
Volunteers

Volunteer Program Interrelationships

Field Office Chief

Field Supervisor

Outreach Workers

PR Advisor

Secretary

Clerical Aides

Newsletter Editor

Writers

Photographer

Admin. Assist.

Director of Volunteers

Tutoring Project Coord.

Tutors

Special Event Coord.

Committee

Researcher

Civic Club President

Members' Planning Group

Unit 1 Supervisor

Unit 2 Supervisor

Case Aides

Corporate Employee Vol. Program Coordinator

In-House Tutoring Coord.

Employee Tutors

Toy Drive Team

☐ = Employee   ◯ = Volunteer

—— = Direct Lines of Supervision

----- = Liaison Lines of Supervision

done down the left-hand side. Then think about who is most logical as a source of help and who needs to be involved for whatever reason. Make a column for each person you plan to involve, whether one or ten. Be sure to have a column for yourself, too, so that you clarify the pieces of the work that you will do. By filling in the resulting Grid, you will have a complete picture of who is doing what to accomplish the total job. Note that there will be empty squares because some team members will only be working on a specific portion of the project, not on everything. Share the completed Grid with each person mentioned on it, so that everyone involved understands how the work is being coordinated.

Time Management

Closely related to the team approach to volunteer management is the broader issue of time management. The better you become at developing systems and procedures that simplify, do several things at once, and save time, the easier you will find your job of managing volunteers. This is also one of the secrets to helping team members work together smoothly.

You can find lots of books and workshops on techniques of time management. Here are just a few tips that seem particularly applicable to the demands of running a volunteer program. As with all such concepts, they are meant as ideals—in real life you can't make hard and fast rules to deal with the unexpected!

- Set aside designated blocks of time for recurring activities and try to do them all at once rather than interrupting yourself throughout the week. So you can schedule interviews with prospective volunteers mainly on Tuesdays (of course being flexible for the person who can't meet your schedule). Or spend the last part of every Friday afternoon on recordkeeping.

- Similarly, consolidate your telephone time. Rather than accepting phone calls whenever they come in, don't talk on the phone during certain hours and then sit down and concentrate on telephone work for other hours. But be sure to return all messages promptly!

- Instead of individual pieces of paper with telephone messages, keep a spiral notebook for this purpose. Record all phone messages as they come in, one after the other. This puts all your call-back names in one place, shows you the sequence of the calls, and works as a log for later reference.

- Make a folder for each member of your management team. During the week, as items arise relating to that team member, stick notes directly into the person's folder. When you have your next progress meeting, all the things you need to discuss are right there—and you don't have to rely on memory.

- Adapt to seasonal time pressures. If there are times of the year during which you can anticipate a larger number of volunteer applications (such as after your organization's major fundraising event or in the fall student rush), change your procedures accordingly. Perhaps you can schedule group interviews during which you provide basic information all at once to several people, and only have to speak briefly with them individually. Or you can offer pre-application orientation sessions—run by an experienced volunteer—to explain the program in detail, distribute application forms, and let prospective volunteers self-screen before having a long personal interview. Later in the year, when the numbers are more manageable, you can return to your preferred system of individualized attention.

- The old, tried-and-true technique of keeping "to do" lists really does work. End each day by taking a moment to list all the things you need to do tomorrow. End each week with a to-do list for Monday. If you are juggling several major job responsibilities, try organizing yourself further by making a separate to-do list for each function. And remember—scrutinize these lists for tasks you can delegate!

Work Area: Develop in-service training options.

Activities	Coordinator of Volunteers	Administrative Volunteers
❶ Solicit needs and interest in in-service training from volunteers and employees; form training committee.	Recruit committee. Give input.	Develop a questionnaire/ survey form.
❷ Plan an annual training schedule.	Finalize schedule.	
❸ Prepare for sessions: invite speakers and other resource people; invite volunteers.	Provide suggestions. Have secretary do mailing to vols.	Research and invite possible speakers.
❹ Conduct or moderate sessions.	Greet people.	Possibly do it.
❺ Evaluate the training.		Develop evaluation tool.
❻ Explore possible ways to collaborate with other volunteer programs to offer additional in-service training.	Make initial contact with counterparts.	Research potential collaborators. Attend collaboration meeting.
❼ Arrange for volunteers to attend special training events, workshops, visit other agencies, etc.		Research oppor- tunities. Coordinate specific events.

Supervision

Experienced Direct-Service Volunteers	Supervisory Staff	Executive Director	Community Resources
Help to administer survey and analyze results.	Make recommendations.	Make recommendations.	
Recommend schedule.	Review suggested schedule to make sure it meshes with employee training calendar.	Review suggested schedule to make sure it meshes with dates of other agency events.	
Make speaker recommendations.	Encourage volunteer attendance.	Recommend speakers.	Agree to speak or serve as resource people.
Be greeters.			Host and conduct some sessions.
Conduct the evaluation.	Make comments and suggestions.	Make comments and suggestions.	
		Suggest possible collaborators.	Agree to attend collaboration planning meeting. Form training cooperative.
Suggest ideas.	Make suggestions and encourage volunteer attendance.	Assist as necessary with formal requests for access.	Offer opportunities.

Supervision

Supervision is a general term that implies many things—individualized training, motivation, praise, constructive criticism, mutual assessment—all necessary to productivity and harmony. Encourage independence in between supervisory meetings with your team members. When a team member has a question, respond promptly, but reinforce your own procedures; if the question really can wait until the next scheduled meeting, say so. Otherwise you weaken the autonomy of your team members.

Make it a rule that no one (including yourself) may give criticism without also assisting with suggested alternatives or solutions. If team members are having a problem, ask them to think up the next course of action. Then it is up to you to back them up. Be sure that team members do not dwell only on problems. Stimulate discussion of what is going well—and give recognition for progress made, as well as for results. (Staff meetings, in-house newsletters and bulletin boards are great places to do this.)

The principle of "self-fulfilling prophecy" is very important to supervision. For the team approach to be successful you must expect success. The higher your expectations, in fact, the more likely you are to motivate the team to succeed.

8

COMMUNICATION STRATEGIES

Yet another element critical to the success of your management team is the effective flow of information. You need to develop workable systems to enable you to remain in contact with your key team members. Given the limitations on your time (and everyone else's), it is important to communicate as concisely, clearly and simply as possible.

If you have to deal with each team member daily or even weekly, you will feel even more pressed for time. But it is not necessary to be so constantly involved. In fact, the whole point is to delegate work and allow independent action. Map out a meeting frequency grid like the one on the next page, which makes it all seem much more manageable.

Obviously you will have to determine the amount of contact that is comfortable and most effective for both you and your team members. It is natural to have to talk more often with a new team member and then build in "separation stages" as the person develops the experience necessary to operate more independently.

Meeting Frequency Grid

	DAILY	WEEKLY	MONTHLY	QUARTERLY	SEMI-ANNUALLY	ANNUALLY	
Office Assistant	X						
Tutoring Coordinator			X				
Researcher		X					
Training Coordinator				X			
Public Relations Staff				X			
Board President						X	
Church Group Liaison					X		
Holiday Planner				X			

Messages and Requests

One concern, especially for a part-timer, is accessibility. There are certain questions that do need your attention quickly, yet you may not be able to drop everything to respond when a team member requests help. One way to utilize team members is to put one of them in charge when you are unavailable. This clearly demonstrates that you have delegated authority as well as work!

Also, consider developing a special Request/Response Form like the one on the following page. Note that this is much more informative than a simple message pad. It guides the user into providing the right information to elicit action from the receiver, avoiding the need for time-consuming clarification. It immediately answers the question: "What do you want me to do?" Similarly, it structures the response so that the necessary work continues to move forward.

When you are not around, having a stack of these forms readily available will enable others to leave you notes in the most helpful format, rather than piling miscellaneous pieces of paper on your desk. Use these forms to make notes while talking on the phone, and after informal meetings to help you follow up with necessary action. Train your secretary or clerical volunteers to take phone messages onto these forms, too.

All team members need a supply of these Request/Response Forms, since the system can and should work both ways. Over time, the accumulated forms become agenda items in supervisory meetings, a record of activity, and documentation of decisions. They can even become part of permanent files, organized either chronologically or by person/subject involved.

This form is especially easy and effective to fax back and forth, allowing a copy for both of you. You can also develop a format like this for use in electronic mail systems.

Project Coordination Matrix

The team approach works best when team members communicate directly with each other without necessarily going through you. This is especially critical for the success of independent projects such as a fundraising event, conference, or gift shop. Developing a "Project Coordination Matrix" allows everyone to cross-check their activities—how they should interrelate with

REQUEST

To: _____   Date: _____

From: _____   Phone: _____

Subject: Fax: _____

- Question or Summary of Issue:

- Action Requested:

- Special Concerns/Deadlines:

- -

RESPONSE

Date: _____

- Answer/Action Taken:

- Explanation:

- Follow Up Needed:

From: _____

Phone/Fax: _____

other team members. It can be created by the team members themselves, a process which builds trust and cooperation in and of itself. The goal is to encourage everyone to consider what they need from each other, and what they will be expected to provide to each other. To ensure that the Grid is utilized by team members, keep referring to it during your contacts with them. Hopefully the habit will catch on and everyone will use it as their roadmap.

The sample on the next two pages gives a Matrix for the coordination of a holiday bazaar. Note how it promotes team work by showing the many two-way transactions necessary to accomplish the final goal.

Here is a simple way to create the Matrix you need. Let's say you have your own holiday bazaar to plan. Call a meeting of the seven sub-committee chairs (program, booths, public relations, etc.) in a room that has an available blank wall and then:

1. Give each team member six pieces of 8 1/2" x 11" paper. At the top of each is the name of a different committee. Each person receives a sheet for the function of every other person on the team— except for their own function.

2. Ask everyone to think about what *his/her sub-committee will need* from every other sub-committee in order for his/her sub-committee to do its piece of the work. Each writes these needs down on the appropriately-headed papers.

3. Now have everyone face the blank wall. Post the names of all seven sub-committees across the top and down the left side. Ask the Program Chair to come up and post his/her sheets across the first horizontal line. Then ask the Booths Chair to do the same on the next horizontal line...and so on. **Read across, everyone can see what each sub-committee** *needs from* **each other sub-committee.**

4. When you are done, **read the columns** *down* **to see what each sub-committee** *must provide to* **each of the others.** You can even discuss necessary deadlines and add them to each square.

	PROGRAM	BOOTHS	PUBLIC RELATIONS
PROGRAM		Need list of booth themes to see if any might suggest tie-in performers; make sure any booths likely to generate noise are far from the stage.	Schedule photo-shoot during rehearsal for press releases.
BOOTHS	Coordinate announcements from the stage to generate audience interest in special booths, prize drawings, etc.		Could use help to come up with booth names that have pizzazz!
PUBLIC RELATIONS	Need schedule of events, bios on performers, press photos.	Need list of all booths. Any special ones of press interest this year?	
TICKET SALES		If you want us to help sell door prize tickets, we need to know now.	Need to know deadlines for publicity.
VOLUNTEERS	Give us volunteer job descriptions, ideal qualifications; schedules needed.	Give us volunteer job descriptions, ideal qualifications; schedules needed. We'll need on-site instruction sheets for each booth.	Give us volunteer job descriptions, ideal qualifications; schedules needed.
FACILITY	Tell us your stage set-up and prop needs; microphone and lighting needs.	A complete list of signs needed; all booth needs: outlets, chairs, etc.	Any special needs?
FINANCE	Submit a list of your anticipated budget needs: itemized expenses anticipated and special requests.	Submit a list of your anticipated budget needs: itemized expenses anticipated and special requests. Also submit projected revenues for each booth.	Submit a list of your anticipated budget needs: itemized expenses anticipated and special requests.

Coordination Matrix

TICKET SALES	VOLUNTEERS	FACILITY	FINANCE
	Need volunteers as stage hands, and for audience control.	Scrounge whatever items we'll need for props; set up the stage and audience area as we request; help with tear-down afterwards.	What is our budget for paying performers?
Need to decide how we will handle door prize tickets.	Will have to arrange a master schedule of volunteers to staff each booth.	Visit site and decide on the number and placement of booths; set up and take down of the booths themselves; lots of signs.	Set revenue goals; set booth item price criteria; solicit donations for door prizes.
Work out advance publicity/ticket sale calendar and last minute sales push. What's the early-bird ticket price?	Need people to put up posters around town; press greeters.	Will need a press greeting area near the entrance, with a telephone.	What's our advertising budget?
	Need people to come into the office to open the mail & fulfill ticket requests; need ticket sellers on site. Will we get volunteers bonded to handle cash?		Decisions about ticket prices and a cash management plan with internal controls.
Give us volunteer job descriptions, ideal qualifications; schedules needed. Let's discuss bonding.		Job descriptions, ideal qualifications, schedules needed. Need a volunteer sign-in area near entrance and a volunteer rest area behind the scenes.	Give us volunteer job descriptions, ideal qualifications; schedules needed.
Any special needs?	We'll need several shifts of work crews before, during and after the event. Make sure volunteers are strong and don't mind getting dirty!		What's our budget?
Submit a list of your budget needs: itemized expenses and special requests. Recommend ticket prices based on last year. Projected sales?	Submit a list of your anticipated budget needs: itemized expenses anticipated and special requests.	Submit a list of your anticipated budget needs: itemized expenses anticipated and special requests.	

5. After you've all had a chance to see and agree on the full Matrix (and copied it down for your own use), remove and redistribute the papers so that each team member receives the six needs lists from everyone present right away. Later you can send a typed version of the complete Matrix to everyone.

This is a wonderful group exercise.[1] It builds the team as it clarifies roles and tasks—and how everything is interdependent. If you do the step of discussing timetables and deadlines, it also becomes clear that different sub-committees are active at different times.

Reporting

Reporting is a more comprehensive type of communication, designed to keep you up-to-date with the status of particular projects, new developments, future plans, and related issues. You certainly don't want to be inundated with tons of paper, but reports can save time (and anxiety!) in the long run when they consist of the right information in the right format. By designing a report form tailored to your situation and need-to-know, you can make the process of reporting relatively painless for your team members—and yourself.

Individual Report Forms can be developed such as the sample on page 98. The form avoids lengthy paragraphs that no one likes to write and you have no time to read. It can be completed by hand with phrases and bulleted lists, and focuses attention on the most necessary information. Each key team member submits a copy to you on a pre-determined schedule (not necessarily monthly). Again, such reports serve as a cumulative record of activity which proves very useful when conducting program assessments, evaluating staff performance and preparing annual reports.

An adaptation of this form facilitates communication among several team members working together on a project. It is especially effective when you have developed a Project Coordination Matrix. On page 99, you will see that the left-hand column of the Team Report Form is the same as the Individual Report Form. The right-hand column allows each team member to communicate progress or questions to other team members related to work they must do together. Ideally, each team member comes to the group meeting with enough copies of his/her report for everyone. This keeps everyone up to date in a consistent, easy-to-read format, and has the added benefit of promoting group and individual accountability.

Committees: Beware!

It is worthwhile to add some words of caution about committees. Committees have been terribly overused as an operational structure and many committees are formed only because it is the traditional way to work on projects. There are plenty of sterling examples of functioning committees, but all too often committees become little more than a series of meetings at which work is only *discussed*. If any work is actually accomplished between meetings, it is usually done by the chairperson—which is one reason for the common response: "I'll be glad to serve on the committee, but don't ask me to *chair* it!" Committees run this way actually dilute responsibility and make it difficult to hold individual members accountable.

The most productive committees are usually ad hoc in nature, since they are formed for a specific, time-limited purpose. If you really want work to get done, call the group a "task force" or "work group"—anything that implies action and results. Then agree on a detailed description of the assignment, a process and a time frame—and let the group loose!

One more suggestion: keep the group to the size best suited to the work to be done. Don't ask six people to be "on the committee" when the job only needs three. In fact, involving only two or three people to focus quickly and easily on a specific assignment may be far more productive than coordinating larger groups. Two or three task force members don't even need as many face-to-face meetings; they can do their planning over the telephone.

Conducting Meetings

Reams of paper and countless hours have been spent discussing the ins and outs of running productive meetings. It can be done! And this is one skill that is critical to maximize the limited time available to you. It is through well-run meetings that you will be able to maintain the interest, motivation and commitment of

Individual Report Form

Report on: _____

Period Covered: _____ Date of Report: _____

Submitted by: _____

- Progress during Period:

- Concerns or Problems:

- Next Steps Planned:

- Other Comments/Questions/Needs:

Team Report Form

Report on: _____

Period Covered: _____ Date of Report: _____

Submitted by: _____

• Progress during Period:	Special information to or questions of other team members:
	To: _____:
	To: _____:
• Concerns or Problems:	
	To: _____:
• Next Steps Planned:	To: _____:
	To *Everyone:*
• Other Comments/Questions/Needs:	

your team members. The key things to remember (whether the meeting is with a group or one-to-one) are:

1. Be prepared. Know what you want to discuss and what decisions need to be made.

2. Announce—and honor—an ending time as well as a starting time. This demonstrates respect for everyone's busy schedule.

3. Develop a written agenda. List the topics in a logical sequence. If you are having a one-to-one meeting, ask the other person to develop a list, too.

4. The first order of business should be to review the agenda(s). Mutually agree to cover those items, in that order.

5. For a group meeting, determine the time available to talk about each agenda item and then stick to it, unless the majority of the group votes to change the agenda.

6. Once a decision is made (whether by vote, by consensus, or by you), do not move to the next topic without also determining:

   – what next steps are needed to act on the decision;
   – who is going to take the necessary action;
   – when the action is to be done.

Depending on the complexity of the issues to be discussed, you might want to ask participants to do some homework in advance (reading reports, talking to each other, generating ideas). Do this sparingly so that when you do request some advance preparation, people will take it seriously.

Minutes

Like committees, minutes are so traditional that they have lost much of their usefulness. Most people hate to take minutes, especially if those pages are rarely read after they are distributed— a lot of wasted effort. Only board or annual meetings require formal minutes for legal purposes. Other meetings (and even parts of board meetings) can be recorded in much more dynamic ways that assist everyone in following up on decisions reached.

A note about making tape recordings of meetings: Only do this if you think someone will listen to them. Remember that replaying a tape takes exactly the same amount of time as attending the original meeting. Does anyone have that much time to spend getting caught up on group discussions?

Instead, consider developing a form which serves as both a *record* of the meeting and an *action plan,* to be used consistently in meetings you chair or in meetings among the various members of your team. A suggested format is on the next page.

Using a form with columns such as these greatly simplifies keeping minutes and provides a much more user-friendly tool for everyone. It places the emphasis on action rather than discussion, and is much easier to scan quickly than paragraphs of narrative. In some situations, the form eliminates the need for a permanent recording secretary. Instead, because the form itself insures consistency, the recording task can be rotated among group members. Even simpler, all members can be given their own blank forms on which to make notes for themselves. If you use the same key words uniformly in the "Subject" column, over time you will have a useful index to track discussion and decisions.

You can add columns that are useful to you. Some examples are: "Resources Needed," "Barriers," and "Who Else Should Be Informed?"

End the meeting by reviewing the items in the last two columns: Is everyone in agreement on next steps to be done and individual assignments? In this way accountability is built in while team members see progress and feel a continuous sense of achievement. Begin the next meeting by reviewing the last two columns from the previous meeting's action plan: Did these steps happen as desired?

If this type of meeting record is reproduced and distributed shortly after each meeting, it will serve as a reminder and guide for both those present and those who could not attend. If you're really pressed for time, ask the person with the neatest handwriting to complete the form during the meeting, photocopy it on the spot, and distribute it before everyone leaves.

Whenever members of your team meet without you or committees meet independently, a copy of their action plan can

Meeting Record: Action Plan

Date: _____   Present: _____

Meeting of: _____   _____

Time Began: _____   _____

Time Ended: _____   Absent (Excused): _____

Minutes taken by: _____   Absent (Unexcused): _____

SUBJECT	SUMMARY OF DISCUSSION	DECISION MADE/ VOTE TAKEN	NEXT STEPS	TO BE DONE BY WHOM/WHEN

automatically be sent to you after the meeting. If every meeting related to the volunteer program uses the same action plan record form, you will stay informed about who has agreed to do what, and when.

By now you may be feeling overwhelmed by forms! But those suggested here serve several purposes at once, being both immediate work organizers and summary documents for your files. Do not duplicate paperwork unnecessarily. For example, if groups or committees utilize the meeting action plan form consistently, there is no reason for additional monthly reports from them. A semi-annual or annual re-cap is all that is needed. Once again, the key is creating a system that does what you need it to do— quickly and effectively.

---

1 Credit for the Project Coordination Matrix concept goes to Christine Franklin who first taught it to us in planning the 1981 National Conference on Volunteer Administration.

CONCLUSION

It may seem as though the suggestions in this Guide will lead you into creating a bureaucracy. This is not the intent. But you are faced with the very real challenge of providing complete leadership of volunteers within a fragmented timeframe. Your only recourse is to get organized and involve others. This does mean systems, forms, and other management tools—but it does not have to mean unyielding rules and regulations. Flexibility, continued enthusiasm, and good human relations skills are just as important to keeping your team productive. You and the team should enjoy running the volunteer program together and taking pride in the results. And if your team really shares authority with you, you will avoid being a bureaucracy since decisions (and adaptations) will be "owned" by many.

Remember the key elements of the team approach:

- Clarify expectations with your top administrators.

- Identify all the pieces of your job.

- Decide what can be delegated.

- Identify potential sources of help both inside and outside your organization.

- Recruit people who welcome an administrative role with the volunteer effort.

- Define the what, how and when for those to whom you are delegating.

- Create an organizational framework that works.

- Establish systems for communicating.

- Share the results with everyone, and celebrate!

Yes, there will be times (especially at first) when the team will not work exactly as planned. You may have vacancies in key positions for longer than you want, or personality conflicts may develop among team members. This is precisely when pulling together is so critical. If team meetings examine how the program is operating as well as focusing on day-to-day task concerns, then possible trouble areas in management can be handled. Again, you are sharing *responsibility*. If a problem arises with the team itself, pose the problem to the team and let members assist in identifying the solution.

When your team participates in tackling difficulties, setting priorities, getting work done, locating resources, documenting results, and visibly moving the organization towards its mission and goals, you will be demonstrating the qualities of a true leader. You will be empowering your co-workers and community members in a way that makes the organization stronger, promotes self-sufficiency and teamwork, and maximizes the impact of volunteer resources.

APPENDIX

Resources to Help You Do the Job

There are many organizations available to help you learn more about the job of managing volunteer programs and link you with your colleagues.

Local Organizations

"DOVIAs"

"DOVIA" is the generic name for "Directors of Volunteers in Agencies" associations but your local group may have a different name, such as Volunteer Directors Roundtable or Council of Volunteer Coordinators. There are several hundred DOVIAs operating in cities and counties across the country. These are associations of leaders of volunteer programs who meet regularly to exchange information and ideas, host workshops and speakers, and plan collaborative activities. The best way to locate such a group in your area is to call your Volunteer Center or contact a director of volunteers in an established organization such as a hospital, literacy program, social service agency or museum and ask if a DOVIA is operating in your community.

Volunteer Centers

There are approximately 500 Volunteer Centers across North America, again with varying names including Volunteer Bureau, Voluntary Action Center, or Volunteer Connection. A large number are part of local United Ways, while others are independent nonprofits or part of local government. Volunteer Centers act as clearinghouses of information to link those who want to volunteer with agencies who are seeking volunteer help. They often sponsor training events, provide consultation to agencies on developing volunteer programs, mobilize citizens for special one-day projects, and coordinate local activities for National Volunteer Week.

State Organizations

Governor's or State Offices on Volunteerism. (Check with your state for exact name, contact person and services.)

Approximately two-thirds of all states have a state government office to coordinate volunteerism in their state. Many serve as a clearinghouse of information, offer training events, publish newsletters, and sponsor conferences and awards programs. The names vary, including Governor's Office of Volunteerism, Office of Citizen Participation, and State Office of Volunteerism and Community Service.

In Canada, several national and provincial departments include publications and technical assistance in volunteer program development as part of their services.

State Associations of Volunteer Administrators. (Names and contacts will vary.)

These are state-level (or provincial-level, in Canada) professional organizations of individuals who lead volunteer programs. Some states have both a State Office and a State Association, while others have one or the other, and some states have neither. State associations generally sponsor self-training events, link members with each other, publish a newsletter, etc.

State Commissions on Community Service. (Names and contacts will vary.)

As a result of 1993 Federal legislation, most states established these Governor-appointed commissions to administer programs funded by the Corporation for National and Community Service. In some states, these commissions are staffed by and work very closely with the existing State Offices of Volunteerism. In other states, the commissions operate as separate entities.

At the second printing, we updated some addresses. Please check the Energize Web site for the most current information: http://www.energizeinc.com

National and International Organizations

Association for Research on Nonprofit Organizations and Voluntary Action (ARNOVA)
c/o Indiana University Center on Philanthropy, 550 West North Street, Suite 301, Indianapolis, IN 46202-3162.
  • Publishes *Nonprofit and Voluntary Sector Quarterly*
  • Annual conference in the fall

Association for Volunteer Administration (AVA)
P.O. Box 32092, 3108 N. Parham Road, Richmond, VA 23294. (804) 346-2266. ava@freedomnet.com
  • Publishes *The Journal of Volunteer Administration*
  • Professional certification program
  • Annual International Conference on Volunteer Administration in October and regional activities throughout the year

Corporation for National and Community Service
1100 Vermont Ave., NW, Washington, DC 20525. (202) 606-5000
  • AmeriCorps, Learn & Serve America, VISTA and other programs
  • All Older American programs formerly under ACTION, such as RSVP, Foster Grandparents, and Senior Companion programs

Independent Sector
1828 L Street, NW, Washington, DC 20026. (202) 223-8100
  • Legislative advocacy, newsletters, research (including commissioning the Gallup Poll on giving and volunteering). Annual conference in October

  Note: The Canadian counterpart is the *Canadian Centre for Philanthropy*, 1329 Bay Street, 2nd floor, Toronto, ON M5R 2C4. (416) 515-0764

National Center for Nonprofit Boards
Suite 510-S, 2000 L Street, NW, Washington, DC 20036.

(202) 452-6262
  • Publications, technical assistance

Nonprofit Risk Management Center
1001 Connecticut Ave., NW, Suite 900, Washington, DC 20036.
(202) 785-3891
  • Technical assistance, publications, training

Points of Light Foundation
1400 I Street, NW, Suite 800, Washington, DC 20005.
 (202) 729-8000. vol net@aol.com
  • Publishes *Volunteer Leadership*
  • Council on Workplace Volunteerism
  • National Council of Volunteer Centers
  • Annual National Community Service Conference in
    June
  • "Volunteer Readership" catalogue (books, recognition
    items)
  • National Volunteer Week materials
  • President's Volunteer Service Awards

Society for Nonprofit Organizations
6314 Odana Road, Suite 1, Madison, WI 53719. (608) 274-9777
  •Publishes *Nonprofit World*

Specialized Organizations

The following organizations link people working in specific settings or concerned with special groups of volunteers such as students doing community service. Many of these are also organized at the state and local level, either through chapters or affiliated associations. All also produce publications and sponsor conferences.

American Association for Museum Volunteers (AAMV)
1225 Eye Street, NW, Washington, DC 20005. (202) 289-6575

American Society for Directors of Volunteer Services (ASDVS)
American Hospital Association, 840 North Lake Shore Drive,
Chicago, IL 60611.

Campus Outreach Opportunity League
1511 K Street, NW, Suite 307, Washington, DC 20005. (202) 637-7004.

International Association for Justice Volunteerism (IAJV)
P.O. Box 7172, Pueblo West, CO 81007. (719) 547-4204.

International Association for Volunteer Effort (IAVE)
c/o Eleanore Schweppe, P.O. Box 546, Old Lyme, CT 06371.

National Association of Community Leadership Organizations (NACLO), 525 W. Meridian St., Suite 102, Indianapolis, IN 46225. (317) 637-7408.

National Association of Partners in Education (NAPE)
209 Madison St., Suite 401, Alexandria, VA 22314. (703) 836-4880.

National Youth Leadership Council
1910 West County Road B, St. Paul, MN 55113-1337. (612) 631-3672

National Society for Internships and Experiential Education (NSIEE), 3509 Haworth Dr., Suite 207, Raleigh, NC 27609.

Youth Service America, 1101 15th St., NW, Suite 200, Washington, DC 20005. (202) 296-2992.

Electronic Forums

Computerized communication networks focused on non-profit issues and volunteer opportunities are developing rapidly, at both the local and national level. For example, many individual Volunteer Centers are developing "homepages" on the World Wide Web or are participating in regional "freenets" to post volunteer opportunities. While cyberspace is changing enormously as this book goes to press, some examples of national electronic forums where volunteerism issues are being discussed are:

CyberVPM Web site and listserv: http://www.cybervpm.com

Formerly "Sound Volunteer Management," this site includes a variety of useful material, including an online introductory course for volunteer management (the "Volunteerism Mini-University"), training and other resources. A real-time chat room is available. Regardless of your level of experience, take advantage of site developer Nan Hawthorne's outstanding listserv, "CyberVPM" (Cyberspace Volunteer Program Management). This free, active electronic bulletin board brings questions and answers from volunteer management colleagues around the world directly to your e-mailbox. To subscribe, send an e-mail to: LISTSERV@LISTSERV.AOL.COM with the message: SUBSCRIBE CYBERVPM<your name>

Energize, Inc. Web site: http://www.energizeinc.com

Focused exclusively on information needed by leaders of volunteer efforts, we offer free access to a library of articles and book excerpts, quotations and parables about volunteering, recognition ideas, a directory of DOVIAs and state associations, a volunteer management job bank, a calendar of conferences and training events, and up-to-date contact information for—and hyper links to—a wide range of international volunteerism resources. The site also has a full Online Bookstore with over 75 books and videos for sale. Every month the site features a new "Hot Topic" essay by Susan Ellis and visitors are encouraged to post responses.

Points of Light Foundation: http://www.pointsoflight.org

This site provides a directory of all Volunteer Centers in the United States, and information on National Volunteer Week, the National Community Service Conference, and other POLF-coordinated activities.

SERVEnet: http://www.servenet.org

A project of Youth Service America, this site offers a great deal of program management information with an emphasis on youth community service and service-learning. Connects to sample programs and awards and offers a weekly electronic newsbrief.

Volunteer Today "Electronic Gazette": http://bigjohn.bmi.net/mba

Another site providing volunteer management information, links, and resources, plus up-to-the-minute "news" items of interest to the field, compiled by trainer/author Nancy Macduff.

BIBLIOGRAPHY

During the past decade there has been a steady increase in the number of publications related to volunteer management. While the following list is by no means intended to be all-inclusive, or even comprehensive, it is a starting point for those newcomers who want learn more. Readers may also want to contact Energize, Inc. at 5450 Wissahickon Avenue, Philadelphia, PA 19144, (800) 395-9800 for the annual "Volunteer Energy Resource Catalog" listing many of these and other additional resources. An asterisk (*) below denotes books available from Energize.

Battle, Richard V. *The Volunteer Handbook: How to Organize and Manage a Successful Organization.* Austin,TX: Volunteer Concepts, 1988.

Ellis, Susan J. *The Board's Role in Volunteer Involvement.* Washington, DC: National Center for Nonprofit Boards, 1995.*

Ellis, Susan J. *The Volunteer Recruitment Book,* second edition. Philadelphia: Energize, Inc., 1996.*

Ellis, Susan J. and Katherine H. Noyes. *Proof Positive: Developing Significant Volunteer Recordkeeping Systems,* revised ed. Philadelphia: Energize, Inc., 1990.*

Fisher and Cole, *Leadership and Management of Volunteer Programs.* San Francisco: Jossey-Bass Publishers, 1993.*

Graff, Linda. By Definition: *Policies for Volunteer Programs.* Etobicoke, Ontario: Volunteer Ontario, 1993.*

MacKenzie, Marilyn and Gail Moore. *The Volunteer Development Toolbox.* Don Mills, Ontario: Partners Plus, 1993.

McCurley, Steve and Rick Lynch. *Volunteer Management: Mobilizing All the Resources of the Community.* Downers Grove, IL: Heritage Arts, 1996.*

Patterson, John with Charles Tremper and Pam Rypkema. *Staff Screening Tool Kit: Keeping Bad Apples Out of Your Organization.* Washington, DC: Nonprofit Risk Management Center, 1994.*

Scheier, Ivan H. *Building Staff/Volunteer Relations.* Philadelphia: Energize, Inc., 1993.*

Stallings, Betty. *Training Busy Staff to Succeed with Volunteers* and the *55-Minute Training* Series. Pleasanton, CA: Betty Stalling & Associates, 1997.*

Tremper, Charles and Gwynne Kostin. *No Surprises: Controlling Risks in Volunteer Programs.* Washington, DC: Nonprofit Risk Management Center, 1993.*

Vineyard, Sue. Beyond Banquets, Plaques and Pins: *Creative Ways to Recognize Volunteers and Staff!* Downers Grove, IL: Heritage Arts Publishing, Revised 1994.

Vineyard, Sue and Stephen McCurley, eds. *Managing Diversity: A Rainbow of Opportunities.* Downers Grove, IL: Heritage Arts Publishing, 1992.

Wroblewski, Celeste J. *The Seven Rs of Volunteer Development.* Chicago: YMCA of the USA, 1994.*

Index

Illustrations

(For enlarging information, see back of contents page.)

About the Authors

Katherine Noyes Campbell currently serves as Director of the Virginia Office of Volunteerism. She has over twenty-two years of experience in the field of volunteerism, both as a program manager and as a trainer and consultant. Noyes Campbell is past president of the Association for Volunteer Administration, the international professional association for leaders of volunteer service programs. She is the author of numerous journal articles and the monograph, *Opportunity or Dilemma: Court-Ordered Community Service.*

Susan J. Ellis is President of ENERGIZE, Inc., an international training, consulting and publishing firm specializing in volunteerism. She founded the Philadelphia-based company in 1977, building on her experience in developing and leading volunteer programs. She is past editor-in-chief of *The Journal of Volunteer Administration* and is recognized for her extensive speaking and writing on the subject of volunteer management. Her books include *From the Top Down: The Executive Role in Volunteer Program Success and The Volunteer Recruitment Book.*

Noyes Campbell and Ellis have enjoyed a close professional relationship for over two decades and have co-authored several books, including *By the People: A History of Americans as Volunteers, Proof Positive: Developing Significant Volunteer Recordkeeping Systems,* and *Children as Volunteers: Preparing for Community Service.*

Other Best Sellers From Energize

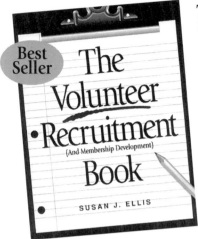

*Energize, second edition, 1996
paperback, 152 pages, 8 1/2 x 11
ISBN 0-940576-18-X,
Catalog #1-128-2, $18.75*

The Volunteer Recruitment Book
By Susan J. Ellis

"...has become the bible of volunteer recruitment!"
-Kerry Tilden, Oxfam International, U.K.

This book is literally crammed with every recruitment suggestion and recommendation the author has developed over her 20-plus years in the field. She shows how to design the best assignments for volunteers as the initial step to finding the most qualified people. She continues by addressing organizational image, where to look for volunteers, why people volunteer or do not, how to select the right recruitment technique, what "diversity" means to an organization, and the impact of trends in volunteering today. There is a complete chapter on membership development for all-volunteer organizations. The second edition contains an appendix on how to use the Internet and other cyberspace opportunities for volunteer recruitment.

From the Top Down:
The Executive Role in Volunteer Program Success, Revised Edition

By Susan J. Ellis,
with sections by Jeffrey D. Kahn, Esq. and Alan S. Glazer, CPA

"The best resource to convince administrators to actively support volunteer programs."
-Jackie Sinykin, Executive Director, The Volunteer Center, St. Paul, MN

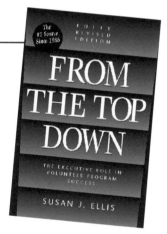

*Energize, Revised 1996
paperback, 210 pages, 6 x 9
ISBN 0-940576-17-1,
Catalog #1-102-2, $21.75*

A best seller since the first edition was published in 1986, this is the first and only book that addresses the top decision-maker's role in a volunteer program. It clearly illuminates the issues necessary to facilitate volunteer program success, including an overall vision, policy questions, budgeting, staffing, employee/volunteer relations, the role of the board of directors, and assessing the impact of volunteer contributions. This fully-revised edition is packed with updated information regarding legal, risk management, and insurance changes; new regulations on accounting practices covering donated time; the growing trend of mergers; and the new categories of stipended and "mandated" community service participants.

Comes with a removable insert with hints on how to get your boss to read it as well!

Be sure you're on our list to learn about resources in volunteerism. Call to add your name: 1-800-395-9800

 **Order Form**

Title	Qty	Price	Total
From the Top Down, Revised		$21.75	
Volunteer Recruitment Book		$18.75	

$ 0-$20 . . . . . . .3.75 $20.01-$50 . . . . . .4.75 $50.01-$100 . . . . .6.50 $100.01-$200 . . . . .9.75 $200.01-$500 . . . .14.25 Over $500 . .To be billed	Total Amount of Order	
	Shipping & Handling (see chart at left)	
	Sub Total	
	PA residents add 6% sales tax; Phila. residents add 7% sales tax	

TOTAL ENCLOSED

____Check or money order, payable to ENERGIZE, Inc. enclosed.
All payments must be in U.S. dollars drawn on a U.S. bank or
as an International Money Order.

____Charge my purchase to: ____VISA   ____MasterCard

Credit Card No. _____

Expiration Date _____

Signature _____

SHIPPING ADDRESS

Please complete...and Print Clearly

Name _____

Title_____

Organization _____

Address (no P.O. Box) _____

_____

_____

Telephone No. (____) _____

E-mail address: _____

Web site address:_____

Send Order and Payment to:

5450 Wissahickon Ave., Philadelphia, PA 19144-5221
or call toll-free **1-800-395-9800**, 9am-4:30pm EST Mon-Fri
In Philadelphia area, call **215-438-8342**
e-mail: **info@energizeinc.com**
FAX 215-438-0434
http://www.energizeinc.com

Collective Wisdom Series to Debut in 1998

Energize has initiated the *Collective Wisdom Series,* which will present the wisdom of savvy volunteer management practitioners on subjects of mutual interest. Each book in the series will bring together the best thinking on a particular topic of those working in the field and their contributions will constitute a major portion of the book. The first book, which will be available in the fall of 1998, will focus on the supervision of volunteers. Despite the variety of innovative supervisory techniques that many leaders of volunteers use everyday, surprisingly little has been published on this vital skill. Call 1-800-395-9800 for details on price and availability.

Energize wants you to be a part of this exciting new book series. Your hands-on, day-to-day experiences managing volunteers are rich with examples and ideas that can inspire other colleagues around the world. Consider sharing them by submitting contributions for future titles in the series.

Energize Web site keeps you on the cutting edge!

Already a favorite site among Internet users interested in volunteer issues, the Energize Web site is continually updated to be useful to you. You'll find:

- A monthly "hot topic" essay by Susan Ellis on an issue of timely interest to leaders of volunteers. And you can join in the dialogue by posting your response and opinion.
- An entire library of articles on volunteer program management.
- An Online Bookstore, with the chance to sample excerpts from more than 65 books on volunteer management.
- Professional education information.
- An up-to-the-minute calendar of conferences and training workshops.
- A DOVIA Directory — at last!
- Quotes and parables celebrating volunteering.
- A volunteer management job bank.

Bookmark it!

Mark the Energize Web site as a "favorite place" and come back often.

http://www.energizeinc.com

". . . your site has been the best and most comprehensive I've found so far. You have saved me literally DAYS of work on the new project our church is undertaking."

Ingrid Skantz, Collegedale Seventh-Day Adventist Church, TN

Receive free e-mail updates about our Web site and publications!
Easy on-line sign-up at:
www.energizeinc.com/fillin/mail.html